Success guides

Intermediate 1 & 2
Modern Studies

Guch Dhillon ✗ Joanne Kerr ✗ Wilma Simpson

Contents

Contents

Welcome to the Intermediate 1 and 2 Modern Studies Success Guide.

About the Intermediate Modern Studies Course

The Intermediate Modern Studies course is divided into three sections with a choice of study themes in each section.

Section A – Political Issues in the United Kingdom

Study Theme 1A	Government and Decision Making in Scotland
Study Theme 1B	Government and Decision Making in Central Government

Section B – Social Issues in the United Kingdom

Study Theme 2A	Equality in Society: Wealth and Health in the United Kingdom
Study Theme 2B	Crime and the Law in Society

Section C – International Issues

Study Theme 3A	The Republic of South Africa
Study Theme 3B	The People's Republic of China
Study Theme 3C	The United States of America
Study Theme 3D	The European Union
Study Theme 3E	Development in Brazil

You will cover at least one theme from each section and you should know from your work in class what study themes you are studying.

Top Tip

You will have to answer one Political Issues, one Social Issues and one International Issues question in the examination. Make sure you are clear about which study themes you have covered.

About Intermediate 1 and 2 Assessments

You should also know whether you will be assessed at Intermediate 1 or 2. You will study the same topics – the difference will be in the questions you will be asked and the amount of knowledge and understanding you will need to show when you answer them.

Questions at Intermediate 1 are worth 4 marks, but Intermediate 2 questions can be worth 4 marks, 6 marks or 8 marks. The sources for evaluating will also be more complex at Intermediate 2 and the Decision Making Task for the Social Issues theme is worth 10 marks.

You can learn more about how to answer Intermediate Modern Studies questions in the Leckie and Leckie book *Intermediate 1 and 2 Modern Studies Grade Booster* by Alan Barclay.

About this Guide

This guide covers all the study themes in Intermediate Modern Studies. Unlike a textbook, it assumes you have already covered a study theme before you use it.

Each study theme is divided into double-page spreads giving you **key** information to refresh your memory for Knowledge and Understanding (KU) questions in your unit assessments (NABs) and the examination. There are also examples of the kind of data you might meet in the sources for Enquiry Skills (ES) questions.

The **Quick Test** at the end of each spread will help you recall and organise the information, give you practice combining written and statistical information and help you to draw conclusions. This should help you to be better prepared for your assessments and the final examination.

There are also **Top Tips** giving you hints about what to look out for, or common mistakes to avoid.

Top Tip

For Intermediate 2 - write as **much detail** as you can when answering the Quick Test questions. Make sure you extract all the information from each written spread and its sources.

The importance of keeping up-to-date

Modern Studies is a constantly changing subject and it is important that your information is as up-to-date as possible. You should aim to use current examples in your answers to gain as many marks as possible.

Using the internet is a good way to find current examples. Use the websites listed on pages 126–127 to help you keep up-to-date. There are links to these websites on the Leckie and Leckie website.

Top Tip

Access useful websites at http://www.leckieandleckie.co.uk

Background

Devolution

A **Labour Government** was elected in 1997 with a **manifesto promise** of devolution for Scotland, Wales and Northern Ireland and held a **Scottish Referendum** (a vote on an issue that usually relates to the constitution) with the following **'double question'**:

1997 Scottish Referendum Results

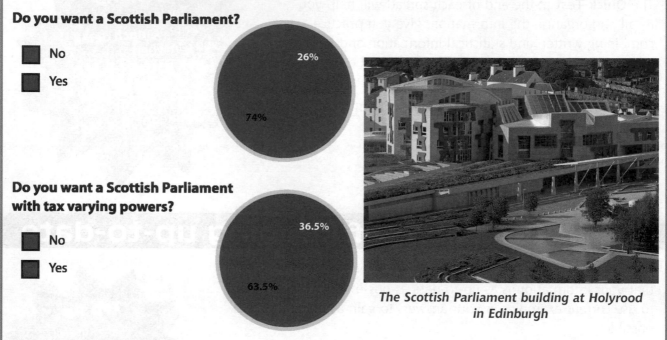

Do you want a Scottish Parliament?

- ◼ No
- ◼ Yes

26%

74%

Do you want a Scottish Parliament with tax varying powers?

- ◼ No
- ◼ Yes

36.5%

63.5%

The Scottish Parliament building at Holyrood in Edinburgh

Source: *Scottish Parliament website*

The result was that in **1999** the **Scottish Parliament** was opened at Holyrood in Edinburgh. The Parliament is sometimes known simply as **Holyrood**.

Arguments For and Against the Scottish Parliament

For	Against
In the 1997 referendum the **majority** of Scottish people voted for devolution.	Some SNP supporters believe that devolution did not go far enough – they want **independence**.
Scotland is a nation with its **own traditions**, culture, and institutions, such as education and the legal system – these all require Scottish political knowledge and control.	Some people argue that Scotland remains at the heart of the **Union** and see devolution as a threat to its strength. There is a **minority** who would like to see the collapse of the Scottish Parliament.
The Scottish Parliament is closer to and more **accountable** to voters.	Westminster and the Scottish Parliament have **clashed** over devolved and reserved powers.
Before devolution the wishes of Scottish voters were **'swamped'** by voters in England – Scotland ending up with a government that did not have the support of the Scottish electorate.	Devolution means that Scots are still governed by Westminster – there is just an **extra layer** of government in-between.

Devolved Matters, Reserved Matters

Definition and Examples

The Scottish Parliament only has the power to deal with issues that affect Scotland – it can deliver 'Scottish solutions to Scottish problems' by passing legislation on Devolved Matters. The House of Commons 'passed down' some of its powers relating to Scotland – these are called **Devolved** Matters, while the **House of Commons** in London has retained **Reserved** Matters to deal with UK wide issues.

Devolved Matters	Reserved Matters
Health Example – ban on smoking introduced in Scotland in 2006.	**Defence** Example – the war in Iraq; Scottish troops are also involved.
Education Example – abolition of student tuition fees.	**Immigration** Example – limits to the number of new migrants; applies to Scotland.
Local Government Example – introduction of the Single Transferable Vote (STV).	**Social Security** Example – introduction of tax credits; also available in Scotland.
Justice, the Courts and the Police Example – harsher sentences for those who commit knife crime.	**Foreign Affairs** Example – agreements to reduce carbon emissions; also apply to Scotland.

The Scottish Parliament has **tax varying powers** of 3p in the pound. Having this power allows the Scottish Parliament to raise money which can then be spent on services in Scotland. However, this power has not been used yet.

Sometimes, the division between these powers can be **blurred** causing real confusion amongst Scottish people and **conflict** between the Parliaments. For example, Scotland currently has a **skills gap** in areas such as dentistry, and therefore needs the skills of foreign dentists. However, immigration is a UK reserved power over which MSPs have very little say.

Top Tip
There is co-operation and conflict between the two Parliaments.

Quick Test

1. What is devolution?
2. What conclusions can be drawn from the 1997 referendum results?
3. Give **one** reason why people are happy with the Scottish Parliament and **one** reason why some people are not.
4. Explain why some matters have been devolved to the Scottish Parliament.

Election Results

Top Tip
For information on **First Past the Post** refer to the chapter on Decision Making in Central Government.

Members of the Scottish Parliament are elected using a **Proportional Representation (PR)** system called the **Additional Member System (AMS)**. Each voter has two votes – one for a political party and one for a candidate. The first vote uses the **Party List System** to elect **56 regional MSPs**. Parties draw up a list of candidates and, depending on the share of the votes they achieve, they are allocated seats. The second vote uses **First Past the Post** to elect **73 constituency MSPs**. The candidate with the highest number of votes is elected.

Scottish Parliamentary Election Results 2003 and 2007

Party	Election results 2003			Election results 2007		
	Regional list MSPs	Constituency MSPs	Total MSPs	Regional list MSPs	Constituency MSPs	Total MSPs
SNP	18	9	27	26	21	47
Labour	4	46	50	9	37	46
Conservatives	15	3	18	13	4	17
Lib Dem	4	13	17	5	11	16
Greens	7	0	7	2	0	2
SSP	6	0	6	0	0	0
Others	2	2	4	1	0	1
Total	**56**	**73**	**129**	**56**	**73**	**129**

Source: Scottish Parliament website

There is a massive difference in the electoral results of **2007 compared with 2003**, not least because Labour no longer hold power in Scotland and there is now a **minority** government instead of a **coalition**. Due to the electoral system employed to elect the Scottish Parliament, it is very unlikely that any party will achieve the **65 seats** needed to achieve a majority. This makes it difficult for any one party to carry out all of its **manifesto promises**. Therefore, it is likely that the current SNP Government will have to be make deals on an **issue-by-issue** basis.

Types of Government

Coalition Government	Minority Government
Some people argue that **coalitions** are a good way of governing Scotland because:	Some people argue that **minority governments** are a good way of governing Scotland because:
• they ensure a more democratic government because the wishes of more people are taken into consideration	• the result accurately reflects the wishes of the public
• they encourage parties to co-operate and share power rather than engage in confrontational politics	• legislation has to be made on an issue by issue basis, resulting in effective co-operation benefiting the Scottish people
• the Cabinet and government will come from a larger pool of people with a greater range of talent.	• the minority government party will have to work hard to gain the confidence and trust of the electorate if they wish to gain re-election.
But... • some people argue that the electorate did not vote for compromised policies, therefore nobody gets what they want.	But... • a minority government is unlikely to be able to put all of their manifesto promises into action.

The Additional Member System (AMS)

Advantages

- The percentage of seats and votes are closely linked, giving a more representative reflection of the wishes of the voters. This system is more **proportional** than First Past the Post.

- In theory, AMS should give **women** and **ethnic minorities** better representation because parties draw up lists of candidates based on merit. This means that the electorate do not have the opportunity to discriminate because they cannot judge the candidates beforehand. Women have benefited as a result of this system because the Scottish Parliament currently has 43 female MSPs – this amounts to around a third of MSPs.

- AMS retains the **link** between MSPs and constituents, giving the electorate a range of representatives to contact should they need assistance.

- **Smaller parties** also benefit because the electorate may choose to give their first (Party List) vote to a party such as the Greens, reserving their second (First Past the Post) vote for the candidate to whom they have greatest allegiance.

Top Tip

AMS has a huge affect on how Scotland is governed.

Disadvantages

- **Coalition** or **minority governments** are likely under this system because it is difficult for any single party will win over 50% of the seats. This means that they do not have a strong **mandate** to govern.

- The List/Regional vote puts **too much power** in the hands of political parties because parties choose who goes where on the list. This may be one reason why ethnic minorities have been continually under-represented in the Scottish Parliament – for the first time in 2007 one ethnic minority MSP was elected in the regional vote. The under-representation of ethnic minorities may be the result of discrimination, or it may reflect the political parties fear that, because of their prejudices, the electorate may not choose a minority candidate.

- Although the link between MSPs and constituents is retained, many people are **confused** about who they should go to with their concerns – should they go to their constituency MSP or their regional MSP?

- AMS can be confusing for some sections of the electorate. This has led to **spoilt ballot papers** and rejected votes. For example, in 2007 over 100,000 ballot papers were rejected.

Quick Test

1. Under the Additional Member System, how many votes does each voter have?
2. Describe **two** advantages and **two** disadvantages of the Additional Member System.
3. What constraints are there on minority government?
4. Explain the difference between a coalition and a minority government.

Scottish Government

Overview

The **Scottish Government** is the name given to the **First Minister**, the **Scottish Cabinet** and politically neutral **Scottish Civil Servants**. The First Minister and Cabinet make decisions for Scotland based on their **manifesto promises**. However, they rely on the other MSPs to vote on legislation so that they can put their promises into action.

Powers of First Minister	Makes the First Minister powerful because ...
Power of Appointment – appoints the Scottish Cabinet and Government Ministers, whips and senior civil servants.	First Minister can reward supporters and not appoint or **reshuffle** (sack or change jobs of) rivals or enemies. If a coalition government is in place then the coalition partners will be rewarded with ministerial roles.
Runs the Government – discusses issues with Cabinet but makes the decisions which become Government policy. Electorate has given the SNP a narrow **mandate** to govern.	Ministers must support a policy in public whether or not they agree with it in Cabinet. This principle of **collective responsibility** gives the impression of unity and strong leadership.
International role – showcases Scotland at international events and **negotiates** with foreign leaders and the UK Government and Prime Minister. However, this influence is limited because foreign affairs is a reserved issue.	**Media coverage** focuses on the First Minister as the leader and positive coverage attracts the support of voters. This can be helpful in giving the First Minister more influence in dealing with Westminster - particularly if he/she belongs to a different party than the Prime Minister.
Majority Leader – leads the largest party in Parliament. Therefore, can push the party's agenda.	Government policies get greater **media attention** than those of the opposition parties.

The Cabinet and Civil Service

The Scottish Cabinet is responsible for government **planning, decision making** and the **legislative programme**. It **co-ordinates** the policies of Government Departments and settles any disputes. The First Minister draws up the agenda and chairs the weekly meeting.

A **Secretary of State** is the lead Minister of a Government Department, with **responsibility** for its policies, legislation and actions. This MSP is expected to have a great deal of expertise and knowledge of their particular department.

Civil servants are **politically neutral** government employees who provide unbiased research and advice to help Ministers make decisions, manage Government Departments and provide services to the public.

Top Tip
The leadership style of a First Minister has a huge effect on his/her popularity.

Power and Limits of the Scottish Government

Examining the work of the Government – the **First Minister** and the **Scottish Cabinet** are members of the Scottish Parliament and are therefore **accountable** to its other members. MSPs ensure that the government performs its duties in the best interests of the Scottish people by participating in:

- **First Minister's Question Time (FMQT)** – **Scottish** Government Ministers must answer questions about the work of their departments. FMQT is every Thursday – when the First Minister has to account for the actions of his government. Leadership weaknesses are often exposed during FMQT, especially when a leader faces pressure from their party and the media.

- **Debates** – MSPs can contribute to discussions on issues that concern their constituents. They can also put forward a **motion** to be debated. These debates can stimulate responses from MSPs, the media and the public.

- **Voting** – MSPs vote using an electronic keypad. AMS has meant that the SNP Government does not have a majority, and therefore relies on the votes of opposition MSPs. The type of government, resulting from AMS, means that whether a government is a coalition or a minority it relies heavily on the support of opposition parties to carry out manifesto promises.

- **Committees** – The Scottish Government is held to account by **mandatory** and **subject** committees who scrutinise proposed bills. Committees perform an incredibly important function by acting as a check and balance to the power of the government. The public are also involved in this process through the **Public Petitions Committee**, which can introduce legislation based on the direct wishes of the public.

- **Making laws** – Scottish Government policies are presented to the Scottish Parliament as **bills** which are debated and voted on to become laws for the government to put into action. There are various opportunities for MSPs to take part in the law making process. For example, MSPs can introduce **Members' Bills** on issues that concern them or their constituents.

- **Funding** – The Scottish Parliament relies heavily on Westminster for funding. This means that the government has to consider the financial implications of making certain policy decisions.

Top Tip

The ways in which MSPs participate can also act to limit the power of the Scottish Government.

Quick Test

1. What are the powers of the First Minister?
2. What is the job of the Scottish Cabinet?
3. What is the role of the Scottish Civil Service?
4. Describe the limits to the power of the Scottish Government.

Local Councils

Responsibilities

Local councils may also be referred to as local government and local authorities. There are **32 local councils** in Scotland. They are responsible for:

- **Providing 'best value'** – Councils must prove that they are sourcing the most cost effective service while providing services of the highest quality. Local councils are responsible for a number of **key services**. These include:

  - **Cleansing and Environmental Health** – refuse collection from homes and businesses, keeping the streets clean and ensuring that the environment is protected. Many local authorities now provide recycling facilities to improve the environment.

  - **Education** – providing a range of educational opportunities for those aged 3 to 18. Additionally, they may also fund further education colleges and nurseries.

  - **Social Work** – providing support for various groups in society, such as children, the elderly and those who may not be able to look after themselves as the result of a physical or mental illness.

  - **Leisure and Recreation** – providing facilities for the general public. For example, authorities may choose to provide libraries and sports centres.

- **Democratic representation** – Local councillors represent people in their local wards by holding surgeries, attending council meetings and voting. They are considered very effective because they understand local problems and issues and are therefore in a better position to resolve problems. In addition, the use of the **Single Transferable Vote** has led to multi–member wards with three or four paid councillors, leading to better representation because the electorate have more choice about whom to contact.

Funding

Local government receives funding from a number of sources. The Scottish Government provides the majority of funding through the **Revenue Support Grant**. This takes into account the population and socio-economic circumstances of an area. Local constituents pay **Council Tax** and local businesses pay **Non-Domestic Rates** (business rates) to their local authority to ensure that local services are delivered to a high standard. The amount of Council Tax charged depends on the value of each property and the number of people over 18 in employment in the household. This is a very unpopular tax that the SNP, and some other political parties, want to replace. In recent years, councils have also looked to the private sector for funding. **Public Private Partnership (PPP)** has enabled many councils to build schools and hospitals that they otherwise could not afford. PPP is a **controversial** scheme because many people feel uncomfortable about the private sector having an input into public services. There are also other drawbacks - PPP schemes mean that there are strict guidelines on how a property can be used. For example, many new PPP schools in Scotland have a limited number of classrooms where wall space, for displays of work is restricted.

Top Tip
Some local councils receive more money than others.

Conflict and Co-operation

Issues

There are a number of issues over which the Scottish Parliament, UK Parliament and local councils have clashed. These issues tend to centre on **money** and **power**. All levels of government want as much money and power as possible; therefore they compete for limited resources – this causes **conflict**. However, there are also areas of **co-operation** which highlight the ability of all levels of government to work together for the greater good.

Conflict has surrounded the following areas:

- **The West Lothian Question** – Scottish MPs at Westminster can vote on issues that affect England, such as health and education, whereas English MPs have no say in equivalent matters that have been devolved to the Scottish Parliament. In recent years this has caused a great deal of conflict – particularly over university tuition fees.

- **Over-representation** – Some people argue that Scotland is over-represented, even although the number of Scottish MPs was cut from 72 to 59, there are still 129 MSPs. Scottish MPs have a reduced **remit**, or workload, but are paid the same as all other MPs. The role of local councils has also reduced since the formation of the Scottish Parliament because much of their former work is now done by MSPs.

- **Funding** – At present, the Scottish Parliament gets its finance from the UK Government as a **'block grant'** determined by the Secretary of State for Scotland. The SNP are demanding fiscal autonomy, where the Scottish Parliament would be responsible for generating money without the support of the UK Government. Some people in England believe that the Scottish Parliament gets too much money from Westminster and therefore they support the SNP's view that Scotland should have fiscal autonomy.

- **Powers** – The SNP believe that the Scottish Parliament should be given more power because of the continuing control by Westminster over reserved matters. They are concerned that Scotland does not have a loud enough voice on UK wide issues. In addition, the SNP also believe that an over-reliance on the block grant makes the Scottish Parliament **subservient** – unable to make the decisions that could improve the lives of the Scottish electorate. However, some argue that additional powers would lead to the eventual break-up of the UK. The UK Government has commissioned a report into the powers of the Scottish Parliament – the findings of the **Calman Commission** may lead to a change in the **distribution** of powers between the two Parliaments.

Quick Test

1. Name **three** things that are the responsibility of local councils.
2. Explain why some services in Scotland are best provided by local councils.
3. From where does local government get its funding?
4. Describe examples of conflict between the UK Government, the Scottish Government and Local Councils.

Pressure Groups

Pressure groups are organisations that strongly believe in an **issue** or **cause**. They aim to **influence** the Scottish Government and get them to take action. Some commentators have stated that pressure groups threaten democracy because they encourage illegal activity and **erode traditional democracy**. Many **outsider** pressure groups break the law in the pursuit of their goals. However, others believe that pressure groups play a **vital role** in modern Scottish society giving an outlet to those who do not have faith in party politics - this is particularly true of Scottish young people. Many young people have turned to pressure groups because they focus on **one** particular area, such as the environment. This contrasts with political parties where stances are taken on a number of issues. As a result of this, and other factors, such as **political sleaze** and **declining trust**, pressure group membership now exceeds that of political parties.

Top Tip
Pressure groups represent people on issues that may be ignored by political parties.

Methods used by Pressure Groups to Influence the Government

Method	Influence
Letter campaign	Members of a pressure group may choose to send letters to the press, local councils and MSPs asking for support. If enough letters are sent representatives may be persuaded to take some action or risk losing votes. **Insider pressure groups** (those that have a close relationship with the government) are more likely to use this strategy.
Petition	Petitions are a collection of signatures of people who feel strongly about a particular issue. They show the extent of public support highlighting public concern about a particular issue. The **Public Petitions Committee** relies on expertise gained from pressure groups to aid decision making and policy suggestions.
Demonstrations	Demonstrations involve people gathering together to express their concern about an issue. They can attract publicity and may force the government to take action to avoid the **media glare**. For example, many people protested against the war in Iraq, despite it being a reserved matter. This inspired MSPs who were against the war to speak out publicly. Many people have commented that this has contributed to Labour's demise in Scotland.

One example of a Scottish pressure group that has used all of the above measures is **Pylon Pressure**. They campaign for electricity pylons to be buried underground so that they do not spoil the beauty of the Scottish countryside.

pylon
pressure

Top Tip
Use the internet to research Scottish pressure groups such as Nil By Mouth and Pylon Pressure.

Media

Newspapers, TV, Radio and the Internet

The media refers to **newspapers, television, radio** and the **internet**. It is a collective term used to describe the way most people get their information about political issues and politicians.

Newspapers do not have to be politically neutral and can give support to one party. People do not usually buy a paper for its political coverage but over time they may be influenced by the position the paper takes. Investigations by **quality newspapers** can reveal misconduct by politicians. Tabloids concentrate on scandals and entertainment which may damage the image of political parties and politicians.

Television must be **politically neutral**, giving balanced coverage to all political parties. Investigative programmes, such as Newsnight Scotland, scrutinise Scottish politicians – holding them to account for their actions.

Ownership of the media is concentrated in the hands of a few companies, such as the **Scottish Media Group**. Media companies tend to support one particular point of view and some people think they may have too much influence. Popular newspapers, such as The Scottish Sun and the Daily Record, often evoke strong political debate on controversial issues.

The Media and Political Parties

Party election broadcasts are used during election campaigns to encourage people to vote in a particular way. Major parties use advertising companies to make short, slick presentations. Increasingly, political parties are using celebrities to publicise their policies and gather support. Political parties, and their **spin doctors**, try to create **sound bites** that will feature in news broadcasts.

Top Tip
The media has a huge impact on political awareness and voting behaviour.

Quick Test

1. What methods do pressure groups use to influence the Scottish Government?

2. In what ways can the media influence public opinion?

3. In what ways do politicians use the media?

4. Explain why some people criticise pressure groups.

The House of Commons

Functions

Representing the people – Members of Parliament (MPs) are elected to act on behalf of the people in their **constituency**. They ask **questions** and **debate** issues in the Commons, **lobby** (try to persuade) Ministers and Departments and examine **legislation**.

Making laws – Government policies are presented to the Commons as **bills** which are debated and voted on to become **statute laws** for the Government to implement. MPs can also introduce **Private Members' Bills** on issues that concern them or their constituents.

Controlling finance – The Commons debates the Chancellor of the Exchequer's **Budget** and approves it as the **Finance Act**. The **Public Accounts Committee** checks the spending of Government Departments.

Examining the work of the Government – the **Prime Minister,** the **Cabinet,** and most other members of the Government are from the Commons and are accountable to its members in the following ways:

1. **Select Committees** – examine and report on the work of the Executive. Hearings are held in public and take written evidence and question witnesses. Committees build up expertise and their reports are debated and reported in media. However, the Government has a majority of its MPs on each committee.

2. **Question Time** – Government Ministers must answer questions about the work of their departments. **Prime Minister's Question Time** is every Wednesday. The Government must publicly defend their actions. MPs can raise constituent's concerns. However, loyal MPs sometimes 'plant' questions and Question Time becomes little more than point-scoring and sound bites.

3. **Divisions (votes)** – the Government requires Commons approval for its laws and other actions. MPs are regularly called to the **division lobbies** to vote. However, the Government usually wins because it has a majority of MPs and **party whip system** ensures that MPs vote with their party.

4. **Opposition** – the second largest party in the Commons provide the **Leader of the Opposition** and **Shadow Cabinet** who hold the Government to account by challenging them in debates, at Question Time and in the division lobbies. The Opposition can call for a **vote of confidence** in the Government. If the Government loses this vote, it has to resign and call a General Election. However, the Opposition have few opportunities because the Government controls parliamentary time and has a majority of MPs in the Commons, who are unlikely to vote their party out of office.

MAKING A LAW

○ **PREPARATION**

— Select Committee

○ **HOUSE OF COMMONS**

— First Reading
Bill introduced to MPs

— Second Reading
Debate on general purpose and vote

— Committee Stage
Detailed examination

— Report Stage
Amendments debated by whole house

— Third Reading
Debate and final vote

○ **HOUSE OF LORDS**

— First Reading

— Second Reading

— Committee Stage

— Report Stage

— Third Reading

— Consideration of amendments

○ **ROYAL ASSENT**

Top Tip
Majority and party loyalty gives the Government the upper hand.

Modernising the House of Commons

The House of Commons has been described as unrepresentative and out-dated and MPs simply 'lobby fodder' for their political party.

The Commons has 646 members; 126 are women and only 15 come from ethnic minorities. The average MP is a 50 year old white male.

MPs vote by dividing into Aye and No Lobbies. As they pass through their names are recorded and counted. When the lobbies are empty the **Speaker** announces the result. There have been calls for electronic voting but MPs like to congregate in the lobbies to do business and discuss matters.

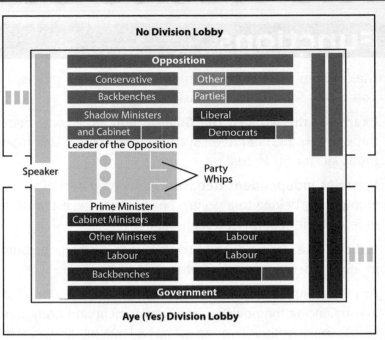

The **whip system** in the Commons means there is little room for MPs to act independently. Whips send a notice (also called a Whip) to the MPs in their party underlined according to importance. A 'three line whip' means MP must attend and vote. An MP who regularly disobeys the whips is unlikely to be re-elected.

There have been some changes to the working practices such as **morning sittings** to make them more family friendly, **three day notice of questions** to make them more topical and **shortening debates** to make them more understandable and easier for the media to report. However, more reforms are needed to make MPs more effective constituency representatives, caseworkers and scrutinisers of the Government.

Job of an MP

MPs divide their time between taking part in the work of the Commons and looking after their constituency. MPs hold **surgeries** in their constituencies where constituents can express concerns. They try to meet as many people as possible by attending functions, giving talks and visiting schools and businesses. MPs are also expected to support their party in the Commons.

Top Tip
MPs may have a conflict of interest between constituency and party and their personal views.

Quick Test

1. What are the main functions of the House of Commons?
2. In what ways can the House of Commons examine the work of the Government?
3. Why do some people think the House of Commons should be modernised?
4. Explain why the House of Commons can find it difficult to examine the work of the Government.

The House of Lords

Functions

Makes laws – the Lords has more time available so it examines, revises and amends bills from the Commons. Some bills also start in the Lords.

Examines the work of the Government – the Lords debate, question ministers and investigate through Select Committees, such as the European Union Select Committee which scrutinises proposals for EU legislation.

Provides independent debate – many Members of the House of Lords (**Peers**) are **crossbenchers** who do not belong to a political party. They have a wide range of expertise and this provides independent debates of a high quality.

Judicial role – the House of Lords is the UK's highest court of appeal. This judicial function will end in 2009 when a separate Supreme Court is set up.

As the second chamber of the UK Parliament, the House of Lords safeguards democracy by checking and balancing the power of the Government and Commons. No party has overall control of the Lords, so when the Government has a large majority in the Commons, it is sometimes the only effective opposition. However, its powers are limited. It can only delay, not stop a law, does not discuss money bills (taxation) and under the Salisbury Convention will pass a bill that was part of the Government's election **manifesto**.

Membership

- **Life Peers** – appointed for their lifetime by the Queen. Political parties make recommendations and the **Appointments Commission** vets them and recommends non-political appointments (**People's Peers**).
- **Law Lords** – full-time professional judges who hear appeals and conduct official inquiries.
- **Archbishops and Bishops** – Archbishops of Canterbury and York plus senior bishops of the Church of England.
- **Elected Hereditary Peers** – until 1999 there were about 700 Hereditary Peers (those with an inherited title). There are now 92 who are elected by fellow Peers to remain until the next stage of the Lords reform.

The debating, revising, investigating work of the Lords is helped by the experience and expertise of its members. However, some people consider that the unelected nature of Peers is out of place in a democracy. They argue that Peers come from a narrow social group and are unrepresentative, restricted in outlook, concentrate on certain narrow issues and have an inbuilt conservative bias. For example, there are only four Labour hereditary Peers.

Top Tip
Lords uses its time and expertise for reviewing, revising and investigating.

Reform of the Lords

The House of Lords and Reformed Chamber

Representation as a % of the whole house

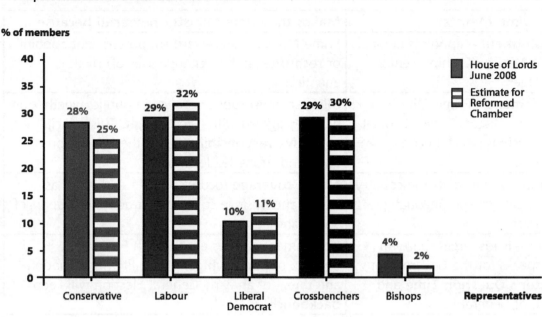

Source: *The House of Lords: Reform, HMSO cm 7027 (Adapted)*

In 2007 a Government White Paper proposed the House of Lords become a 'reformed chamber' with:

- A 'hybrid' of elected and appointed members
- A reduced size from 746 to 540 members
- An end to hereditary and life peerages over time but keeping Church of England bishops
- Elected members voted at same time as Euro elections using proportional representation system with party list reflecting diversity of UK population
- Mixture of party and non-party figures as appointed members
- Every five years one-third of seats to be up for election and appointment
- Maximum of 15 years in office. Members cannot stand for re-election or appointment
- Commons would still have dominance – Lords would revise and scrutinise.

However, there is disagreement about how reform of the Lords should proceed. MPs have voted in favour of an 80%, or wholly, elected second chamber, but Lords have voted for an appointed second chamber. If there is to be an element of appointment, the Public Administration Select Committee wants no suspicion of 'cash for honours'. They want parties to submit a list of justifications why someone should be appointed and to end the right of the Prime Minister to approve recommendations.

Quick Test

1 What are the main functions of the House of Lords?
2 In what ways are the powers of the Lords limited?
3 What reforms are proposed for the House of Lords?
4 Explain why the House of Lords is being reformed.

The Executive

The Prime Minister

Powers of the Prime Minister	Makes the Prime Minister powerful because ...
Power of Appointment – appoints Cabinet and Government Ministers, whips, senior civil servants, judges.	Prime Minister can reward supporters, not appoint or **reshuffle** (sack or change jobs of) rivals or enemies.
Runs the Government – Prime Minister is 'first among equals'. Discusses with Cabinet but makes the decisions which become Government policy.	Ministers must support policy in public, whether or not they agreed with it in Cabinet. This principle of **collective responsibility** gives the impression of unity and strong leadership.
International Role – represents the country at international meetings and negotiates with foreign leaders.	**Media coverage** focuses on Prime Minister as leader and positive coverage attracts the support of voters and party.
Majority Leader – leads largest party in the Commons, speaks for the Government at **Prime Minister's Question Time** and chooses the date of General Election.	Government policies get through Parliament because of **party whips**; possibility of promotion and threat of an early General Election will keep **backbenchers** loyal.
Executive Head – in charge of **Civil Service** and oversees all Government Departments through the **Cabinet Office** and Prime Minister's **Private Office**.	Prime Minister is only member of the Government with an overall view and can use staff, advisers or **Cabinet Committees,** rather than full meetings, to direct policy and enhance leadership image.

Limits to the Power of the Prime Minister

Cabinet – to keep the party united, the PM often has to pick rivals. A Cabinet with policy disagreements, resignations or scandals can damage the reputation of the Prime Minister.

Parliament – Government MPs can stage a **backbench revolt** and amend or defeat Government legislation. The Opposition can call for a **confidence vote.** Weak performances at **Prime Minister's Question Time** can damage the Prime Minister's leadership image.

Party – MPs can vote against a Government policy, or if the **voters** turn against a Prime Minister there may be a **leadership challenge** by members of parliamentary party who want a new leader before the next election.

Media – the Prime Minister gets more media attention than rest of the Government. Weaknesses or mistakes are widely publicised and negative press damages standing with party and voters.

Top Tip

P = Power of Appointment
R = Runs the Government
I = International Role
M = Majority Leader
E = Executive Head

The Cabinet

The Cabinet is responsible for government **planning, decision making** and **legislative programme**. It **co-ordinates** the policies of Government departments and settles any disputes. The Prime Minister draws up the agenda and chairs the weekly meeting. The Cabinet does not vote; instead the Prime Minister sums up 'mood of the meeting' and records this as the decision. Much of the work is done by **Cabinet Committees** appointed by the Prime Minister who also decides who will sit on them. The Cabinet is expected to accept committee decisions and this has led to the charge that Cabinet simply agrees to decisions already taken.

Job of a Cabinet Minister

Most Cabinet Ministers have the rank of **Secretary of State** – the head of a Government department with **ministerial responsibility** for its policies, legislation and actions. They are expected to resign if mistakes are made, although this happens less now than it used to. They offer proposals and advice to Cabinet and Cabinet Committees. They act as **Front Bench spokesperson** for the Government and department in debates and **Ministerial Question Time,** and they promote party and Government policy in the media.

Civil Service

The Civil Service provides the staff to run the Government. It is **politically neutral**; it serves whatever party is in power according to the **Civil Service Code** of integrity, honesty, objectivity and impartiality. Its job is to provide unbiased research and advice to help ministers make decisions, manage Government departments and provide services to the public.

However, the role of the Civil Service has changed. The majority of civil servants now work for **executive agencies** that deliver Government services. The Government employs its own **special advisers** on policy and **spin doctors** to get its message across to the media. This has led to concerns that Civil Service is being overruled or **politicised** by having to consider political consequences of a course of action.

Top Tip
The Civil Service provides the impartial advice. The Cabinet takes the political decisions.

Quick Test

1. What are the powers of the Prime Minister and how are these limited?
2. What is the job of a Cabinet?
3. What is the role of the Civil Service?
4. Explain why the Prime Minister is more powerful than other Government Ministers.

Participation

People can participate in decision making by **voting** in a **General Election** to elect a Member of Parliament for their constituency. They can also contact their MP by telephone, letter and email, or personally **lobby** them at their **surgery** or House of Commons to make their views known. A lot of participation is through organisations such as **political parties** and **pressure groups** where a group of people can also use their power, and the **media,** to influence decision making.

Political Parties

People join political parties to take part in forming **policies** (proposals about how the country should be run). Members of political parties select candidates for, or stand as a candidate themselves, in General Elections. They also raise money for election expenses and campaign to get candidates elected by putting forward their views and encouraging people to vote. Each political party has an **ideology** (set of views) which is used to develop its policies and the **manifesto** (programme for government) it presents at election time. Parties with a left wing ideology believe the state should distribute wealth more evenly and those on the right believe the individual should provide for themselves. Traditionally, SNP and Labour are thought to be on the left, Conservatives on the right and Liberal Democrats in the centre. However, there is an increasing trend for parties to have a **populist** approach where they find out what people want and adopt policies accordingly. This has led to claims that there is now very little difference between the policies of the main parties.

First Past the Post Election System

At least every five years, those eligible can vote to choose their MP in a **General Election** using **First Past the Post** (Simple Majority) system. The UK is divided into **646** areas called **constituencies**. The candidate with the most votes wins the constituency (or **seat**). The party with most MPs (seats) in the Commons forms the Government. The usual result is a **Majority Government** where the winning party has more MPs than all the other parties put together. This gives stability, accountability and choice. The Government can get policies through the Commons without having to rely on the votes of other parties or go into a **coalition** with a smaller party. The official opposition holds the Government accountable and provides an alternative at the next election.

Ballot paper	
VOTERS British citizens over 18 on Electoral Register but not Members of the House of Lords, prisoners and some psychiatric patients.	
CANDIDATES British citizens over 18, nominated by 10 electors, pay deposit of £500.	
VOTING Place an X in box next to name of candidate you want to vote for.	X

Top Tip
The party system is necessary to provide a Government and an official Opposition.

Arguments about First Past the Post

The 2005 General Election results show some of the strengths and weaknesses of the First Past the Post system.

Governing party has a majority.

Winner got more seats than votes.

2005 General Election results

	Candidates	Votes	Seats	% of seats	% of votes	% of electorate
Labour	627	9,552,436	355	55.0	35.2	21.6
Conservative	630	8,784,915	198	30.6	32.3	19.9
Liberal Democrat	626	5,985,454	62	9.6	22.0	13.5
SNP	59	412,267	6	0.9	1.5	0.9
Others	319	1,205,630	25	3.9	9.0	44.1
Total	2261	25,940,702	646	100	100	100
Turnout	61.4%					

1 in 3 of the electorate did not vote.

Smaller parties got more votes than seats.

Only 1 in 5 voted for the Government.

Source: Political Science Resources, Keele University (Adapted)

Strengths of First Past the Post

- **Strong Government** – outright winner, not dependent on support of other parties. The winning party can carry out the programme it promised the voters.
- **Representative** – voters can express views on which party they want to form the Government. There is a strong relationship between MP and constituency.
- **Simple** – easy to understand and administer. The result is known within a few hours. It has worked for a long time.

Weaknesses of First Past the Post

- **Unfair** – governments can get elected with only a small amount of public support. More people usually vote against the Government than for it.
- **Wasted votes and tactical voting** – votes cast for losing candidates do not count in seat allocation. Many people vote to keep out a candidate they dislike.
- **Lack of choice** – smaller parties get a lot of votes but very few MPs. Government tends to be provided by either Labour or Conservative.

There have been calls to reform the election system for the House of Commons by introducing **Proportional Representation** (PR).

Top Tip
See **Additional Member System** in Study Theme 1 for an example of a PR system.

Quick Test

1. In what ways can people participate in decision making?
2. How do political parties help people to participate?
3. What are the strengths and weaknesses of the First Past the Post election system?
4. Explain why the winning party in a General Election will prefer to be a majority government.

Non–Participation in Political Activity

Decline in Participation

Participation in formal political activity has decreased in recent years. The **membership** of the major political parties has fallen. The Conservative Party has a quarter of the members it had twenty years ago and the Labour Party has half.

This decline also applies to **turnout** in General Elections which has fallen from over 70% in the 1980s to an all time low of 59% in 2001. Some groups - the young, those on lower incomes and ethnic minorities - are becoming increasingly disengaged from politics. Turnout amongst young people is about half that of adults. More 18-34 year olds voted in 2004 *Big Brother* final than in 2005 General Election.

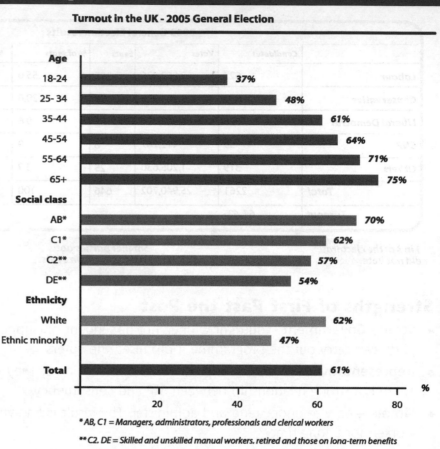

Turnout in the UK - 2005 General Election

Age	
18-24	37%
25-34	48%
35-44	61%
45-54	64%
55-64	71%
65+	75%

Social class	
AB*	70%
C1*	62%
C2**	57%
DE**	54%

Ethnicity	
White	62%
Ethnic minority	47%

| Total | 61% |

AB, C1 = Managers, administrators, professionals and clerical workers

**C2, DE = Skilled and unskilled manual workers. retired and those on lona-term benefits*

Source: *Election turnout, 2005, Electoral Commission (Adapted)*

Reasons for Low Turnout

Among the reasons for low turnout are:

- declining interest in politics
- lack of trust in politicians whom people expect to spin and manipulate
- little difference between the parties so it does not matter who wins
- result with First Past the Post is often a foregone conclusion. People know who will win so do not have a sense that their vote counts
- voting in person–at polling station is inconvenient for some people.

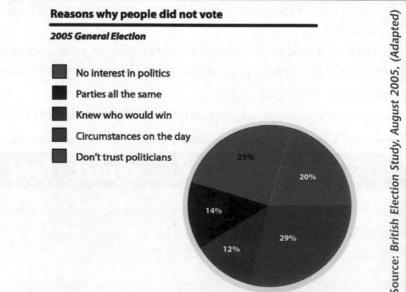

Reasons why people did not vote

2005 General Election

- No interest in politics
- Parties all the same
- Knew who would win
- Circumstances on the day
- Don't trust politicians

25%
20%
14%
29%
12%

Source: British Election Study, August 2005, (Adapted)

Attempts to Increase Participation

Attempts to increase participation have included lowering the age of candidates to 18 and voting by post. Over 5 million **postal ballots** were issued in 2005 General Election and they had a high turnout of 76%. There have also been experiments with text and computer voting and using more convenient locations such as supermarkets. Other suggestions to increase turnout include **weekend voting,** replacing party political broadcasts with **advertisements,** encouraging more **independent candidates** by reducing the likelihood of lost deposits, **compulsory voting** and **positive abstention**. A 'none of the above' option would be included on ballot paper for people to register their disapproval. There have also been suggestions that turnout could be increased by replacing First Past the Post with a **Proportional Representation** system.

However, the membership of **pressure groups** is increasing and people are more willing to participate in this kind of political activity. Pressure groups do not contest elections or want to form the Government, but they do want to influence government policy.

Top Tip
See Study Theme 1 for more information about pressure groups.

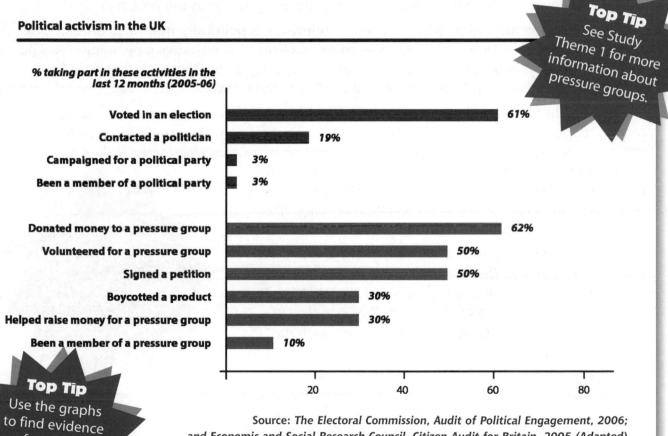

Political activism in the UK

% taking part in these activities in the last 12 months (2005-06)

- Voted in an election — 61%
- Contacted a politician — 19%
- Campaigned for a political party — 3%
- Been a member of a political party — 3%

- Donated money to a pressure group — 62%
- Volunteered for a pressure group — 50%
- Signed a petition — 50%
- Boycotted a product — 30%
- Helped raise money for a pressure group — 30%
- Been a member of a pressure group — 10%

Source: *The Electoral Commission, Audit of Political Engagement, 2006; and Economic and Social Research Council, Citizen Audit for Britain, 2005 (Adapted)*

Top Tip
Use the graphs to find evidence of, and draw conclusions about, participation.

Quick Test

1. Which groups had the highest and the lowest turnout in 2005 General Election?

2. What are the reasons for low turnout?

3. What could be done to try to improve turnout?

4. What **conclusions** can be drawn from the graphs on pages 24 and 25 about the level of political participation?

Influence of the Media

Newspapers, TV, Radio and the Internet

The media - **newspapers, television, radio** and **internet** - is the way most people get their information about political issues and politicians. Now that the traditional factors of social class, job and family background are less important, the media is the main influence on voting behaviour. The media is also the 'eyes and ears' of the people, who can use the **Freedom of Information Act** to access to information and scrutinise the government.

Newspapers do not have to be politically neutral and can give support to one party. People do not usually buy a paper for its political coverage but over time they may be influenced by the position the paper takes. Investigations by **quality newspapers** can reveal misconduct by politicians, and the **tabloids** search for scandals which can damage the party as well as the politician.

People are more influenced by what they see, so **television** is **politically neutral** and has to give balanced coverage. However, television does cover problems in investigative programmes, and put politicians under pressure in interviews. Satirical comedy programmes that comment on current events can also influence people's opinions of politicians and parties.

The **ownership** of the media is concentrated in the hands of a few companies. Media companies tend to support one particular point of view and some people think they could have too much influence on how people vote. At election time, Trinity Mirror Group (*The Mirror, Daily Record, Sunday Mail, Sunday People*) and Guardian Media Group (*The Guardian, The Observer*) supported Labour. DMGT (*Daily Mail, Mail on Sunday* and a share in *ITN News*) and Press Holdings (*Daily Telegraph, Sunday Telegraph*) supported the Conservative Party.

The biggest and most powerful media company is News Corporation who own *The Times, Sunday Times, The Sun* and the *News of the World* as well as a large share of *Sky Television. The Sun* is the newspaper with the largest circulation in the UK. It is estimated that over 8 million people read a copy each day. In 1997 News Corporation and *The Sun* changed their support to Labour who have won the last three general elections.

Top Tip
According to Ofcom, in the 2005 General Election television was the main source of information for nine out of ten voters.

Controls on the Media

Some government information is too sensitive or could put the country in danger and is **censored**. The **Official Secrets Act,** which all government employees sign, means that sensitive information cannot be disclosed for thirty years. The **Press Code** sets out guidelines for the media to behave responsibly and not invade people's privacy.

If this is broken, people can contact the **Press Complaints Commission** who will investigate. If the media print or broadcast incorrect facts they can be sued for **libel** (printed) or **slander** (broadcast). The Government has tried to reduce the influence of large media corporations by restricting **cross-media ownership**. Companies have a limit to the stake they are allowed to have in different branches of the media.

How Political Parties use the Media

Political advertising is not allowed on television but parties who have candidates in one-sixth of the seats are given airtime for **party election broadcasts**. The major parties use advertising companies to make short, slick presentations. During a general election campaign all the major parties hold early morning press conferences at which they highlight a particular policy and criticise rival parties. They try to create **sound bites** that will feature in news broadcasts.

Politicians are trained in use of the media, including how to speak, look and dress. They use interviews, appearances on programmes and newspaper columns to get their message across.

Over half the households in the UK have internet access and political parties use websites, blogs, podcasts and social networking to connect with voters.

Political parties have special departments and spin doctors to handle their image and put their message in the best light, although this has backfired in recent years. On the 11th September, 2001, the day the Twin Towers in New York were attacked, Jo Moore, a Labour spin doctor in the Department of Transport sent an email to colleagues suggesting that it would be good day to bury bad news because it was unlikely to get noticed. When this was discovered she had to make an apology and eventually resigned.

Top Tip
Parties employ spin doctors to put their message across to the media.

Quick Test

1 In what ways can the media influence opinion?

2 What controls are there on the power of the media?

3 How do politicians use the media?

4 Explain why the way newspapers can influence the political system is sometimes criticised.

The Welfare State

Overview

The Welfare State, set up by the Labour Government of **1945-1951,** aimed to address the massive inequalities in health and wealth in Britain. By **1948** it was fully established when it included the **National Health Service (NHS)**. Although the Labour Government are credited with establishing the Welfare State, the Liberal Government of 1906–1911 laid the foundations.

> **Top Tip**
> The Welfare State is unique to Britain.

The Welfare State in Britain exists to provide people with **social** and **economic support** in times of need. **The Beveridge Report** – written by Sir William Beveridge in 1941 – outlined **'five giants'** that caused inequality in Britain, and suggested solutions that would involve the government taking the lead in defeating the 'giants':

- **Disease** – ill health. The report recommended the establishment of a **National Health Service.**
- **Want** – poverty. The report recommended the creation of a **social security** system.
- **Ignorance** – a lack of education. The report recommended **reform** of the education system.
- **Idleness** – unemployment. The report recommended the implementation of policies aimed at creating **full employment** in Britain.
- **Squalor** – poor quality housing. The report recommended a programme of **house building** that would increase council house stock.

The Welfare State faces many **challenges** in modern Britain, not least because the system was not designed to cope with the demands that it now faces. As time has passed, the 'giants' outlined by Beveridge have not been solved. In fact, in recent years, inequalities between those who are wealthy and those who live in poverty have **increased**. The majority of the country's wealth is now controlled by the wealthiest **ten percent** of the population. At the same time, the cost of the Welfare State has increased dramatically, reflecting the fact that the poorest fifty percent of the population own less than ten percent of the wealth.

In 2007–08 total public spending was around £589 billion. This works out to be approximately £9,700 for every person in the UK. It will rise to around £617 billion in 2008-09, £647 billion in 2009-10 and £678 billion in 2010-11.

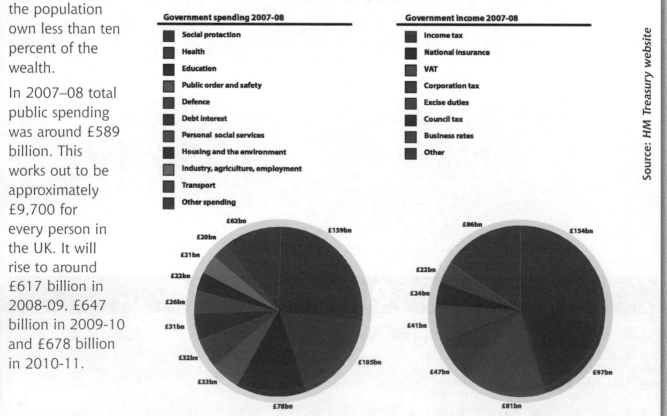

Government spending 2007-08

- Social protection
- Health
- Education
- Public order and safety
- Defence
- Debt interest
- Personal social services
- Housing and the environment
- Industry, agriculture, employment
- Transport
- Other spending

£62bn, £20bn, £21bn, £22bn, £26bn, £31bn, £32bn, £33bn, £78bn, £159bn, £105bn

Government income 2007-08

- Income tax
- National insurance
- VAT
- Corporation tax
- Excise duties
- Council tax
- Business rates
- Other

£86bn, £22bn, £24bn, £41bn, £47bn, £81bn, £154bn, £97bn

Source: HM Treasury website

Poverty

Definitions of Poverty

It is important to understand that there is a difference between **income** and **wealth**. Income refers to the money that people earn from work or investments, or claim as benefits. Wealth refers to the ownership of assets such as property, shares and savings. **Poverty** is about more than a lack of income and wealth. It is about a **lack of opportunity,** or **life chances,** which results in a low income and poor living standards. There are several definitions of poverty and there are several ways of measuring it. The two main definitions of poverty are **absolute poverty** and **relative poverty.**

Absolute poverty is a life-threatening situation where a person has no access to the necessities they need to survive. The United Nations lists these necessities as food, safe drinking water, sanitation, shelter, health and education and considers that poverty depends "not only on income, but also on access to services." A person would be considered to be living in absolute poverty when they have no access to necessities that they need to survive.

Relative poverty is a **lack of equal access** to things that the society in which a person lives considers to be necessary. For example, if a person lives in a developed country like Scotland but does not have a washing machine, bed, cooker, etc then they would be considered to be living in relative poverty.

Over time a society's view of poverty and acceptable standards of living change. This happens for a number of reasons. One reason is that when housing, education and income **improves,** so does health.

The Households Below the Average Income (HBAI) scale, Income Support Levels and the Poverty and Social Exclusion Survey are used to **measure poverty**, but these measures are not always accurate because there are so many variables involved. Some measurements consider weekly income, while others examine perceptions of poverty – asking a sample of the population to define what they consider to be essential to a decent standard of living.

Top Tip
Background to the Welfare State will not be examined, but it is essential that you understand it.

Quick Test

1. Why was the Welfare State established?
2. What is the difference between relative and absolute poverty?
3. What challenges does the modern Welfare State face?
4. Why is it difficult to measure levels of poverty?

Causes of Poverty

There are numerous factors that cause poverty. Factors that **cause** poverty may also end up being **consequences** of poverty. Many people in Britain are trapped in a **vicious cycle of poverty.**

Top Tip
Most of the factors that cause poverty are also consequences of poverty.

The Vicious Cycle of Poverty

Although the UK is a wealthy country there are massive gaps in wealth between the richest and poorest people in society – this gap is currently **increasing**.

Unemployment and Benefits

One of the most significant causes of poverty is unemployment. This is because if jobs are limited more people will rely on **benefits** such as Job Seekers Allowance, and these benefits only provide limited amounts of money for claimants. The benefit system is designed to encourage people to find work by only providing enough money for a very basic standard of living. This is a problem because some people will suffer from long term unemplyment and will not be able to sustain a decent standard of living. In Britain about **5%** of those eligible to work are currently unemployed. A number of factors influence unemployment figures, including the **global economy** and the **collapse of traditional industries**, such as coal mining and shipbuilding.

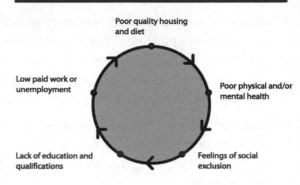

Vicious cycle of poverty

Poor quality housing and diet

Low paid work or unemployment

Poor physical and/or mental health

Lack of education and qualifications

Feelings of social exclusion

Low Pay

Coupled with unemployment, low pay is a major cause of poverty. Many people work in industries where they are only paid the National Minimum Wage (NMW), and therefore struggle to meet their needs. Many employees who earn the NMW are females, who work part-time in low skilled jobs. If these women are also lone parents then they, and their children, are vulnerable to poverty.

Family Structure

Lone parents are more vulnerable to poverty than other family types as they are reliant on the wages, or benefits, of only one adult. The majority of lone parents in Britain are female.

Gender and Race

Discrimination has lead to some of the inequalities experienced by ethnic minorities and women. However, as time progresses, this is likely to become less of a factor because attitudes will change. Therefore, it will be other issues that will have an impact on these groups. For example, women are likely to have lower incomes because they are concentrated in more poorly paid jobs in the service sector (hospitality and catering) and the public sector (education and social work).

Despite social change, women still tend to occupy the role of carer. This has an impact on career progression because many women may choose not to aim for the highest jobs because of family commitments. It may also be the case that employers do not give women the same opportunities because they assume that they will not be able to cope with the demands of their position.

Some ethnic minority groups also experience inequality as a result of racial discrimination placing barriers in the way of success and career progression. The culture of a particular minority group and emphasis placed on education have a huge effect on poverty. The stronger the family structure, and value placed on education, the less chance there is of poverty.

Consequences of Poverty

Poverty causes a huge range of problems for those who experience it, and for the country as a whole because the **economy** suffers when there is a high level of **economic inactivity** and **reliance** on the benefit system. When a person lives in poverty there are many consequences; these can **trap** a person in poverty and even worsen their situation.

Mental and Physical Health Problems

Mental and physical health problems are often suffered by those in poverty. The rising incidence of **depression** in Britain illustrates the effect that poverty can have on an individual's mental and physical wellbeing. With approximately **one in six** adults suffering from depression or anxiety this has led to depression being labelled a '**silent epidemic**'. Depression is both a mental and a physical illness because it can impair a person's ability to work and conduct a 'normal life'. Many people experience depression as a direct result of feeling hopeless and helpless about their lack of opportunities; this is **social exclusion**. These feelings may also lead some people to abuse alcohol and smoke heavily – both of which can have a huge impact on health and life expectancy.

Social Exclusion

At the heart of social exclusion is a lack of income, but it goes further than this. It is also about power and powerlessness and a lack of hope and expectation. This may lead to a lack of educational, or work, success and a repetitive **pattern of failure**. Unfortunately, this has led to Britain having the highest suicide rate in Europe for young men.

Inequalities in Education

For many families living in poverty education is not a priority – not because parents do not value the potential of their children, but because there are more pressing problems of how to provide, and pay for, basic necessities such as shelter and food. As a result, the education of children suffers and **aspirations** and **expectations** remain low. This can result in the generational repetition of poverty as families struggle to break the cycle.

Poor Quality Housing/Homelessness

In many instances a lack of income leads to a lack of good quality housing, and in extreme cases this may lead to homelessness. Poverty can be witnessed all over major British cities in run-down '**sink estates**' where crime rates and drug abuse are high and health problems are common.

Quick Test

1. Explain why unemployment and low pay might lead to poverty.
2. Why might women and ethnic minorities be vulnerable to poverty?
3. Why is ill health often a consequence of poverty?
4. What is social exclusion?

Tackling Poverty

The government and other agencies have put many policies and benefits in place to help those vulnerable to poverty. These aim to address financial, employment and training needs. Many of the policies put in place by the Labour Government are collectively known as **'Welfare to Work'**. The aim of welfare to work schemes is to ensure that unemployed people are as employable as possible.

Benefits can be broken into two groups – **universal** and **means-tested**. Universal benefits are those to which all people, in certain circumstances, are entitled to irrespective of income/wealth. Examples are child benefit and the state pension. Means-tested benefits involve individuals meeting certain criteria; they are targeted at those with low or no income. For example, to claim Job Seekers Allowance (JSA) a person must be actively seeking employment.

Help for the Unemployed

Financial	Employment	Training
Income to help meet needs.	Help finding a job or another source of work.	Develop skills and gain qualifications.
National Government provides –		
Job Seekers Allowance (JSA) A benefit paid to the unemployed who are **actively seeking employment**. The amount varies depending on individual circumstances (whether a person is single, a lone parent or married with children, etc.).	**New Deal Phase 1** New Deal clients start with an interview at the local Job Centre Plus. A **personal adviser** will help them by arranging help with: • applying for jobs • attending interviews • drawing up CVs. **New Deal Phase 2** If the person is still unemployed after **four months**, other options are discussed: • self-employment • voluntary work • environmental task force • full-time education. There are different types of New Deal for various groups (New Deal 50+, New Deal for Lone Parents etc.).	**Skillseekers** People aged 16 – 18 are placed on a scheme which provides a mixture of skills training and work experience. They have to join to qualify for benefits. Some Skillseekers may be kept on by a company after the training period has ended. **Modern Apprenticeships** These are aimed at school and college leavers, taken on by an employer and paid a wage or an allowance. The aim is to give the apprentice qualifications and work experience.
Local Government provides –		
Council Tax Benefit This is a reduction in council tax. **Housing Benefit** This is a rent reduction.	**Libraries** provide newspapers and free internet access to allow people to find and apply for jobs.	**Learning Centres** provide training in word processing to help people produce CVs and application forms.
Other help		
Voluntary groups such as the **Citizens Advice Bureau** provide information about applying for benefits. Unemployed people can also work for voluntary groups to gain some work experience and skills.		

Help for the Unemployed and Low Paid Individuals

National Government	Local Government	Other
Child Benefit A universal benefit paid to all families with children, not affected by savings or income.	**Housing Benefit** A means-tested benefit that assesses a person's ability to pay rent.	**Private companies** Provide services such as child-minding and private nurseries.
Tax Credits Child Tax Credit and Working Tax Credit are available to ensure families are better off in work than on benefits.	**Council Tax Benefit** A reduction in the amount of Council Tax paid.	**Voluntary organisations** Citizens Advice Bureau counsel families on claiming benefits, dealing with debts etc. The Child Poverty Action Group campaigns for better family benefits so poorer families can have a better standard of living.
	Nurseries Child and after-school care are provided at low cost to families with a low income.	**Child Support Agency (CSA)** The CSA traces absent parents and fixes an amount for them to contribute to the upbringing of their children.

National Minimium Wage (NMW)

The Labour Government introduced the National Minimum Wage to set a minimum hourly wage rate. From October 2008 this is £5.73 per hour for workers over 22. Younger workers have a lower minimum. The NMW has helped to lift many people out of poverty. However, many people do not believe that the rate is high enough to provide a real solution to poverty.

Top Tip
You should use the internet to keep up-to-date with current benefits. One useful website is Directgov.

Quick Test

1. Describe the difference between universal and means-tested benefits.
2. What opportunities does the New Deal offer people to improve their skills and become more employable?
3. What are the advantages of the financial, training and employment opportunities offered to unemployed people by the government?
4. Describe two policies put in place by the government to help families and low paid workers.

Causes of Health Inequalities

Since the introduction of the National Health Service in 1948 health service provision in Britain has improved. However, despite the dramatic **increase** in life expectancy and **decrease** in disease there are still factors that cause inequalities. Without doubt there is an **clear link** between inequalities in health and wealth.

Top Tip

Although all of the information below is true, you must avoid making generalisations about groups of people in society.

Lifestyle

Poor lifestyle **choices** lead to a poor standard of health. The abuse of alcohol and drugs, smoking, poor diet and a lack of exercise all contribute to a poor level of health and exposure to disease.

In areas with high levels of **socio-economic inactivity** (high unemployment and high levels of low paid, low skilled work) poor lifestyle choices are more prevalent. This explains the impact that geographical location can have on health.

Geographical Location

Within some British cities there is a massive gap in health. In the Glasgow area alone there is a huge gap of around **28 years** in life expectancy between Lenzie and Calton. This gap relates mainly to inequalities in wealth. In the most affluent areas lifestyle is better as is access to health service provision.

Social and Economic Disadvantage

Social and economic disadvantage generally relates to poverty. Studies have consistently shown that there is a strong **correlation** between poverty and ill health. People with a higher income have more control over their destiny because they can afford to make good health choices. They can do this because greater wealth provides them with greater life chances, such as access to good quality education and perhaps the ability to afford private health care.

Environment

The area in which a person lives can have a huge impact on health. If an area is **deprived** there is a significant increase in problems that relate to poor quality housing, such as **asthma** and **bronchitis** – both of which can be caused, and be made worse, by damp. However, this is not the only impact that deprivation can have – it may also increase the likelihood of poor lifestyle choices by young people. These choices can further feed the vicious cycle of poverty; a pattern that can be repeated down the generations. The **visual perception**, or look, of an area can lead to a sense of hopelessness and, for many people, can be a factor that leads to **depression**.

Age

As people age their bodies begin to **deteriorate**. This deterioration can be worsened by poverty and poor lifestyle choices. Health problems increase with age and elderly people over the age of **85** are more likely to suffer from illnesses, such as arthritis, heart disease, Alzheimer's and hypothermia.

Some elderly people can afford to pay for private health care with quick access to treatment and are likely to have shorter spells of ill health. However, the majority of elderly people cannot afford private health care.

Gender and Race

Men are **less likely** than women to regularly attend their doctor for **health check-ups**. One result of this is that women have a greater life expectancy than men. However, men are becoming more comfortable with taking an active role in their own health and wellbeing. This may be the result of high profile **government campaigns** to raise awareness of problems such as testicular cancer.

Cultural differences between ethnic groups account for differences in health problems. For example, in some cultures women are taught to be modest about their bodies, which may result in them attending their GPs less often and not engaging in physical activities. Women and ethnic minorities are more likely than white men to be concentrated in low paid, low skilled work, encountering health problems that are associated with poverty.

Top Tip

Health and wealth inequalities are linked. In areas with high levels of deprivation, there is a greater number of people with health problems and lower than average life expectancy.

Quick Test

1. Explain why people living in deprived housing schemes are more likely to have health problems.
2. Explain the link between income and health.
3. Describe the ways in which poverty affects many people.
4. What impact does age have on health?

The National Health Service – NHS

The NHS employs more than **1.5 million people**. Of those, just under half are medically trained, including approximately 90,000 hospital doctors, 35,000 General Practitioners (GPs), 400,000 nurses and 16,000 ambulance staff.

The number of patients using the NHS is huge and increasing all the time. Approximately **1 million patients** use the NHS every **36 hours**. Every week around 700,000 people visit their NHS dentist and in the same time period each GP will treat around 140 patients. In the last 60 years advances in technology, medicines and clinical practice have meant that costs have soared.

Funding

In 1948 the NHS had a budget of **£437 million** but by 2007/8 it received ten times this amount – more than **£90 billion**. A large percentage of this money is passed to local health authorities who can choose to spend the money as they see fit. This means that severe health problems in an area can be targeted.

Health care is divided into two categories; **primary** and **secondary**. Primary care includes health services that play a central role in the local community, such as GPs, pharmacists and dentists. These are the services that most of us use on a regular basis. Secondary care refers to more long-term medical treatment that we may associate with hospitals. This care is typically provided in local hospitals, usually on referral from a GP or another health professional.

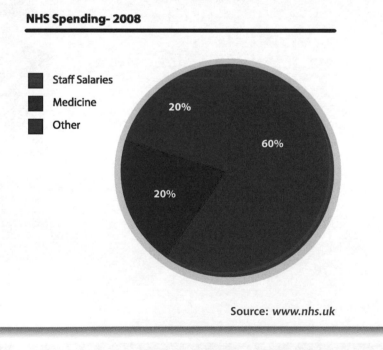

NHS Spending- 2008

- Staff Salaries
- Medicine
- Other

20%
60%
20%

Source: *www.nhs.uk*

Features of Primary and Secondary Health Care

Primary health care	Secondary health care
GPs – Provide a wide range of health services, including: • advice on health problems • examinations and treatment • vaccinations • prescriptions for medicines • referrals to other health services.	Accident and Emergency – A&E departments assess and treat people with serious injuries and those in need of emergency treatment. They are often referred to as **casualty departments**.
Dentists – Provide a wide range of oral health treatments, including; • advice on oral health problems • examinations and treatment • prescriptions for medicines • referrals to other health services.	Care of the elderly – Health care treatment for those who are elderly and perhaps have age related illnesses.
Opticians – Provide a wide range of services, including: • carrying out eye tests to check vision and eye health • examinations and treatment • referrals to other health services • prescribing and fitting glasses and contact lenses.	Maternity – Health care treatment for those who have perhaps experienced problems during pregnancy and for those who are in labour. However, throughout pregnancy women will also attend a midwife as part of their primary care.
Pharmacists/chemists – Experts in medicines and how they work, who provide a wide range of services, including: • dispensing prescriptions • giving advice on general health problems The SNP Scottish Government have unveiled plans to abolish prescription charges in Scotland by 2011.	Paediatrics – Health care treatment for children.
Mental health services – Initially, many people with minor mental health problems will go to their GP.	Mental health services – More specialist mental health care provision; perhaps for those with the most severe mental health problems.

Care in the Community

Elderly people are now encouraged to stay in their own homes as long as possible with the support of a number of services. Social workers assess their needs and draw up a **care plan** to meet these needs using the services listed below:

Day Care Centres and Lunch Clubs

Elderly people can attend these and transport will be provided. Balanced meals are provided at a low cost, reducing the food costs incurred by the elderly person.

Home Support Workers

Home support workers (also known as 'home helps') provide a range of vital services, including cleaning, shopping, washing and ironing, as well as providing much needed company, advice and emotional support.

Community Nurses and Occupational Therapists

Community nurses provide basic health care. Occupational therapists supply equipment, such as grab rails, special baths, showers and remote controlled alarm systems to improve the quality of a person's life.

Positive and Negative Features of Care in the Community

Positive Features	Negative Features
Independence is retained because the person can continue to live at home and family members are able to contribute to the care of their relatives. Meets the needs of some elderly people because they have their own **care plan** which identifies what they need and who will provide the care.	Some elderly people who remain in the community suffer injury and declining health because their needs have been inappropriately assessed or they have 'slipped through the net'. Many elderly people would be better placed in residential care. It is argued that some elderly people, who should be in residential care, are kept in the community because it is a **cheaper option**.

Care in the Community is also used to support the **disabled** and those with **mental health problems**.

Quick Test

1. Why has the cost of the NHS massively increased in the last 60 years?
2. Name the two types of care provided by the NHS?
3. Explain why community care is better for some people while residential care is better for others.
4. Name three features of community care.

How Health Needs are Met

Health needs are met by all levels of government and various outside agencies, including volunteers and private companies. Approaches taken by the government are based on the principles of **individualism** and **collectivism**. This means that the government accepts that some factors that affect health are outwith an individual's control. However, each individual is encouraged to take responsibility for the factors that they can control.

Top Tip
The government aims to improve the health of the nation by tackling **attitudes** towards diet, alcohol and drug abuse and exercise.

Scottish Parliament

The Scottish Government's aim of making Scotland **a better, healthier place for everyone, no matter where they live** has led them to implement initiatives to encourage healthier lifestyle attitudes and choices. They have worked in partnership with **NHS Scotland** to reduce the number of people who smoke, drink excessively and have a poor diet.

The Scottish Government has implemented healthy eating and exercise programmes in schools, such as **'Health Promoting Schools'**, to discourage pupils from eating **'junk foods'** that are high in fat, salt and sugar and encourage them to take part in physical exercise. Many schools no longer sell sweets or fizzy drinks.

It is thought that these programmes will act as a long term solution to health problems because good lifestyle habits learned in childhood will improve health and increase life expectancy by reducing **heart disease** and **obesity**.

Councils

As part of the **Schools (Health Promotion and Nutrition) (Scotland) Act 2007** all 32 Scottish local councils have a responsibility to ensure that health promotion is at the heart of school life. This means that the meals provided for pupils should be **nutritionally balanced**. To ensure that this happens many local councils have put 'swipe cards' systems in place that remove the stigma attached to receiving a free school meal.

In addition to this, North Lanarkshire Council has created several **Sports Comprehensives** – the aim being to raise the standard of achievement and level of participation in physical education, sport and physical activity for all students across a range of abilities.

Private Sector

For those who have a high disposable income, or who have private health insurance, the **private health sector** can meet needs and ensure speedy treatment. There are now many private companies, such as BUPA, who provide care for those who are willing to pay. This is not the only way that the private sector meets health needs – it also does this through the **Public Private Partnership** scheme. This scheme allows the Scottish Government and councils to build new assets, such as hospitals, by using money from private companies. These are then leased over a set period of time. This meets health needs because it improves hospital buildings and equipment, providing a higher level of service delivery for patients.

Quick Test

1. Explain what the government has done to meet health needs.
2. Describe the ways councils aim to meet health needs.
3. What does the private sector do to meet health needs?
4. Why is education important in tackling health inequalities?

Crime

A **crime** is any action which breaks the formal laws of a society and for which a person can be punished. The laws of Scotland are made by the UK Parliament and the Scottish Parliament and enforced by the police and the legal system.

> **Top Tip**
> See Study Themes 1 and 2 for information about how laws are made.

Types of Crime

- **Crimes against the person** – **violent crimes**, such as murder, assault, rape and extortion which involve the threat, or use, of physical force. They also include **culpable homicide** where someone is unintentionally responsible for someone's death e.g. through driving dangerously or under the influence of drink or drugs.

- **Crimes against property** – **dishonesty**, such as housebreaking, theft and shoplifting; **vandalism**, such as deliberately causing damage or setting fires.

- **'Street' crime** – **alcohol related crimes** such as drunkenness, breach of the peace and assault; **drug related crimes** such as possessing, supplying and theft to pay for the habit; **car crime** such as vandalism, theft from vehicles or stealing vehicles. These types of crime are often linked together to create a pattern of crime. The increasing use of weapons has led to concern about **gun and knife crime**.

There is general **consensus** (agreement) that these types of crimes are serious, but public opinion is often divided about other types of crime such as:

- **Minor offences** – speeding, littering, smoking in a public place or underage drinking are not considered crimes by many people.

- **White collar crimes** – tax evasion, fraud or embezzlement are less visible and often committed by experts of a high social status.

- **Corporate crimes** – dumping waste, breaking health and safety laws or making misleading claims are often difficult to prove.

- **Organised crime** – the drug trade, sex industry, protection rackets, illegal gambling or counterfeiting by people who make their living from crime.

- **Political crime** – bombings and other acts of terrorism in support of a cause rather than for personal gain.

Crimes and offences recorded by the police in Scotland (2006/07)	
Crimes of violence	14,009
Crimes of indecency	6,726
Crimes of dishonesty	183,760
Vandalism and fire raising	129,734
Drugs	42,422
Offensive weapons	10,110
Other Crimes	32,406
Motor vehicle offences	375,033
Miscellaneous offences	232,373
Total crimes and offences	**1,026,663**

Source: Recorded Crime in Scotland, 2008, Scottish Government (Adapted)

Why Some People Commit Crime?

Economic Reasons

We live in a **materialistic society**. Status is measured by what people own and to appear 'normal' people require certain possessions. People who are **unemployed** or on **low income** often lack the means to acquire these legally. Even when people have what appears an adequate income, 'status frustration' – envy or jealousy of the quality of life of others – can lead to crime.

Some people are **professional criminals** who make their living from organised crime. The **drug trade** – importing, manufacturing and selling of drugs and the associated gang crime – is almost an alternative economy in some areas.

Social Reasons

Learned behaviour – family break-ups, absent fathers, poor role models and fewer poor 'respectable' communities lead to 'amended values' with different ideas of 'right and wrong' in which crime becomes 'normal'. For young people **peer pressure, boredom** and a **rejection of 'adult' values** can lead to crime for thrills where it is seen as smart, tough and exciting.

Environment – rural areas and suburbs have fewer social problems than inner city areas and 'sink' estates. **Deprivation, social exclusion** and a **lack of facilities** in these areas has led to alienation, where some people, particularly the young, feel cut off from mainstream society and do not see much advantage in obeying its rules. **Drug and alcohol abuse** is higher in these areas which often leads to crime being committed while under the influence or to pay for the habit.

Quick Test

1. What is the definition of a crime?
2. What are the main types of crimes?
3. Give reasons why some people commit crime.
4. What conclusions can be drawn about the amount and type of crime recorded in Scotland?

Alcohol

Licensing (Scotland) Act, 1976

Age limit of 18 to buy alcohol and 16 to buy beer, wine or cider with a meal. Licence holder can refuse sale to anyone under age of 21.

Local Government (Scotland) Act, 1973

Local authorities can introduce bye-laws banning drinking in public places.

Crime and Punishment (Scotland) Act, 1997

Police can confiscate alcohol from underage drinkers in public places.

Licensing (Scotland) Act, 2005 (in force from 2009)

No proof, no sale – must have proof of age to buy

Responsible sale – must not serve people who are drunk

No 'happy hours' – prices must be set 48 hours in advance

Illegal to buy alcohol for under-18s – £5000 fine and/or 3 months prison sentence

Proposed Changes

The Scottish Government is considering measures to curb binge drinking, including:

- raising the minimum age to 21 to buy alcohol in off licences and supermarkets
- fixing a minimum price for alcohol, banning cheap promotions and retailers being charged a 'social responsibility fee' to help with cost of alcohol misuse – £2.25 billion a year (£500 for every adult in Scotland).

Should the Legal Age for Buying Alcohol be Raised to 21?

For	Against
Reduce anti-social behaviour by making it more difficult for very young teenagers to buy alcohol.	Will increase illegal drinking on street corners and parks.
Reduce alcoholism and other effects of alcohol in young people by delaying age at which they can buy alcohol.	Not able to enforce current laws which many young people ignore and the number drinking alcohol is rising.
Reduce the number of crimes fuelled by alcohol.	Shows lack of trust in young adults who are old enough to marry at 16 but not considered mature enough to make a sensible decision about alcohol.
Reduce the number of road traffic accidents due to alcohol.	Many young people drink socially and do not develop serious problems. Many European countries have a lower drinking age and fewer problems.

Tobacco

Tobacco Advertising and Promotion Act, 2002

Banned tobacco advertising and sponsorship.

Smoking, Health and Social Care Act, 2005

Banned smoking in enclosed places from 2006 and raised the legal age to buy tobacco products to 18 from 2007. Retailers can be fined up to £2500 for selling cigarettes to under 18s.

Proposed Changes

The Scottish Government is considering measures to:
- licence tobacco retailers
- ban behind counter displays, introduce plain packaging and stop sale of packs of ten cigarettes
- crack down on smuggling and counterfeiting.

Should Licensing of Tobacco Retailers be Introduced?

For	Against
Reduce outlets for purchasing tobacco. Licensing system, similar to alcohol, would reduce sales, prevent addiction and reduce effects of smoking.	Smoking not reduced e.g. in France and Spain level of smoking remained the same. More difficult to enforce than alcohol which has separate licensed premises.
Reduce illegal sales to young people. Enforcement of age limit is poor. Retailer would have to ask for proof of age or face fine or loss of licence.	Young people can get tobacco from other sources such as over-18s or illegal suppliers who may also deal in other drugs. Increase in criminal activity like smuggling and counterfeiting.

Top Tip
Laws on alcohol and tobacco are changing. Use the internet to keep up-to-date.

Quick Test

1. List the main points of the current laws on alcohol and tobacco.
2. What changes to these laws are proposed?
3. Give the main arguments for and against licensing tobacco retailers.
4. Explain the main arguments for and against raising the legal age to buy alcohol.

Controlled Drugs

Misuse of Drugs Acts, 1971

It is an offence to possess, supply or intend to supply a controlled drug, or to allow premises to be used for drug taking. Drugs classified as Class A, Class B and Class C.

Proceeds of Crime Act, 2002

Scottish Crime and Drug Enforcement Agency can seize assets of convicted drug dealers.

Anti-Social Behaviour Act, 2004

Police can enter and close down premises used for drug-taking.

Misuse of Drugs Act, 2005

Reclassified cannabis from Class B to Class C and toughened sentences for dealing.

Punishments for possessing and dealing drugs	
Class A (e.g. cocaine, heroin, ecstasy, LSD)	Up to 7 years in prison and/or unlimited fine for possession; up to life in prison and/or fine for dealing.
Class B (e.g. speed, amphetamines, Ritalin)	Up to 5 years in prison and/or unlimited fine for possession; up to 14 years in prison and/or fine for dealing.
Class C (e.g. cannabis, tranquillisers, Ketamine)	Up to 2 years in prison and/or unlimited fine for possession; up to 14 years in prison and/or fine for dealing.

Proposed Changes

The Scottish Government is considering measures to:

- reclassify cannabis from C to B again
- target growing and supplying of cannabis and ban the sale of drug taking equipment
- give harsher sentences for those caught supplying near schools.

Should the Government Reclassify Cannabis?

For	Against
More potent 'skunk' is the most common type of cannabis in Britain. Produced by intensive indoor cultivation and three times stronger than ten years ago.	Less harmful than alcohol and tobacco. Criminalises medical users, whereas other countries allow use of cannabis e.g. Canada licenses a cannabis mouth-spray for multiple sclerosis sufferers.
Increased cannabis use since given lower classification. Some evidence that it is addictive and linked to psychotic and other mental illnesses, particularly in teenagers. Increase in the number of convictions for driving under the influence.	Dispute over the link to mental illness. Advisory Council on the Misuse of Drugs' found little evidence that cannabis is associated with major health or sociological problems.
Keeping it at lower classification makes step into drug taking easier. Cannabis can be 'gateway' drug that can lead onto harder drugs like cocaine or heroin.	Britain has toughest laws, yet highest use. Waste of police time – better to chase the dealers and focus on more harmful drugs like heroin and cocaine.

Traffic Offences

Road Traffic Acts 1988 and 1991

Driving without tax or MOT: maximum £1000 fine.

Driving without licence: 3-6 points on driving licence, maximum £1000 fine, possible disqualification.

Driving without insurance: 6-8 points, maximum £5000 fine, possible disqualification.

Speeding on non-motorway: 3-6 points, maximum £1000, possible disqualification.

Speeding on motorway: 3-6 points, maximum £2500 fine, possible disqualification.

Refusing breath test: 4 points, maximum £1000, possible disqualification.

Driving with excess of alcohol or drugs: 4 points, maximum £5000 fine, disqualification.

Failure to stop and/or report an accident: 5-10 points, maximum £5000, possible disqualification.

Road Safety Act, 2006

Driving while using hand-held mobile phone – 3 points and £60 fine

Causing death while unlicensed, disqualified or uninsured – 2 years in prison

Causing death by careless or inconsiderate driving – 5 years in prison

Proposed Changes

The UK Government is considering introducing a graduated licensing scheme:

- not taking driving test until 18
- complete minimum number of lessons and hazard perception training before taking a tougher test
- zero alcohol limit for one year after taking test
- ban on carrying passengers aged 10 to 20 from 11pm to 5am for one year after test.

Raising the Legal Driving Age?

For	Against
Reduce the number of deaths. 1000 deaths a year. 1 in 3 drivers killed are under 25. Rises to 1 in 2 at night.	Reduces mobility. 70% of 17 year olds drive themselves to work. Car vital in rural areas for freedom and independence.
Stop young drivers over-estimating their skill. Over-confidence, exuberance, alcohol, drugs and peer pressure to drive dangerously.	Difficult to enforce and only postpones the problem. Accidents are due to inexperience, not age.

Quick Test

1. List the main points of the current laws on drugs.

2. What changes to these laws are proposed?

3. Give the main arguments for and against raising the legal age for driving.

4. Explain why some people believe the current law on cannabis should be changed.

Top Tip
Laws on Drugs and Traffic Offences are changing. Use the internet to keep up to date.

The Police

The main roles of the police in Scotland are to protect the public, keep law and order, prevent crime and detect criminals. Scotland has eight police forces (Central, Dumfries and Galloway, Fife, Grampian, Lothian and Borders, Northern, Strathclyde and Tayside). There are over 16,000 police officers, serving as a constable, sergeant, inspector, chief inspector, superintendent, assistant chief constable or chief constable.

Police forces have:

- **uniformed branch** with foot and mobile patrols in radio communication with their control room
- **Criminal Investigation Department (CID)** detecting crime, preparing crime statistics, advising on crime prevention and usually with a specialist drugs unit
- **Traffic Department** enforcing road traffic laws, managing traffic and dealing with accidents
- **specialised departments** like underwater units, mounted police, police dogs and community involvement.

Police Powers

- Stop and question a suspect or witness.
- Search a person suspected of having an offensive weapon, stolen property or drugs or of being a terrorist.
- Detain a person at a police station for six hours for questioning.
- Arrest a person and charge them with a crime they see them committing or for which they have reliable witnesses and evidence.
- Enter a building with a warrant or without one if they hear a disturbance, are pursuing a criminal or suspect it is a drug den.
- Use reasonable force in pursuit of their duties.
- Issue Fixed Penalty Notices.

Terrorism

Various **Terrorism Acts** from 2000 to 2006 ban certain organisations, widen the definition of terrorism to include praising, encouraging, planning, preparing or training for terrorism, allow **control orders** against suspected terrorists that restrict their movement and ban access to the internet and give the police power to detain suspects for 28 days without charge, with plans to increase this to 42 days. These powers of detention give police greater powers to gather evidence from computers and overseas, as well as question terrorists. The Government also wants to introduce **Identity (ID) Cards**. However, opponents argue this takes away our civil liberties and does more harm than good because it builds up resentment and leads to more terrorist recruits.

CCTV

Closed circuit television in town centres, businesses and mobile police surveillance cameras record criminal activity and allow police to identify and charge more offenders. Those in favour of CCTV argue that people feel safer and there is less crime because criminals are more likely to be caught. However, some people argue that crime simply moves to areas without cameras and that cameras are an invasion of privacy.

Community Policing

Community policing, or neighbourhood policing, is when the police and the community work together to identify problems of crime and solve them. Police became more isolated from the community because the need for an instant response led to use of police cars and radio communication. People feel safer with police officers on foot patrolling a 'beat' and getting to know local people.

Police can work with other agencies, such as social work, education, youth groups and neighbourhood watch. However, this does rely on the public taking an active part by reporting incidents and being witnesses and with increased specialisation there are fewer police officers available for foot patrols.

Top Tip
Some people think police officers on patrol are more effective than CCTV cameras. Be prepared to discuss this.

Increase Police Numbers

More police on patrol could cut crime. Only one-third of police are available to patrol or attend an incident, the rest are involved with paperwork, meetings or court preparation. The level of the 'night-time economy' and increased duties like dealing with anti-social behaviour, managing sex offenders and anti-terrorism means a bigger demand for police. However, recruiting new officers has proved difficult and there is no guarantee that numbers alone will cut crime.

Taser Guns

Trained firearms officers can use taser guns to give a 5-second, 50,000 volt electric shock to disable a suspect. They are considered safer than using firearms and there are calls for these to be distributed to all police officers to combat violent street crime. However, use of taser guns in America has resulted in 130 deaths and there are claims that arming all police will undermine the trust between the police and the community.

Scottish Police Services Agency (SPSA)

The SPSA provides support services like criminal records, forensic services, Scottish Police College and Scottish Crime and Drug Enforcement Agency across the whole of Scotland. The Justice Committee of Scottish Parliament report on police resources has recommended services like firearms, air support, motorway policing, serious crime investigation and counter-terrorism be provided nationally to remove duplication of services and allow local police forces to concentrate on reducing crime and disorder in the community. However, local police forces believe they should retain all their powers because they are accountable to local people and know their area best.

Quick Test

1. What are the main powers of the police?
2. In what ways has the threat of terrorism changed the powers of the police?
3. Give arguments for and against community policing and more police on the 'beat'.
4. Describe the role of the police in Scotland.

Scottish Court System – Criminal

Procurator Fiscal

After the police charge someone with a criminal offence they send the details to the Procurator Fiscal who looks at the evidence and decides whether or not to go ahead with the prosecution. The Procurator Fiscal also inquires into sudden or suspicious deaths and fatal accidents.

Procedure

There are two types of procedure:

- **Summary** – trial before a sheriff, stipendiary magistrate or justice of the peace without a jury, used for less serious offences.
- **Solemn** – trial before a sheriff or judge with a jury, used for serious offences.

Scottish Criminal Courts

Scottish Court of Criminal Appeal
Judges from the High Court of the Justiciary hear appeals.

High Court of the Justiciary
Most serious crimes e.g. murder, rape, armed robbery, drug dealing.
Solemn procedure with judge and jury.

Maximum Penalties
Unlimited fine - life imprisonment.

Sheriff Courts
More serious offences e.g. theft, assault, possession of drugs.
Summary procedure with Sheriff alone or solemn procedure with Sheriff and jury.

Maximum Penalties
Summary - £10,000 fine - 12 months imprisonment.
Solemn – Unlimited fine - 3 years imprisonment.

Justice of the Peace Courts
(replacing District Courts from 2008)
Minor offences e.g. breach of the peace, petty theft, drunk and disorderly.

Summary procedure with Justice of Peace (JP) alone. JP is not a lawyer, but has trained Legal Clerk for advice.

Maximum Penalties
£2,500 fine - 60 days in prison.

Top Tip
Sheriff Courts handle both criminal and non-criminal (civil) cases.

Scottish Court System – Civil

Scottish Civil Courts

Civil courts settle disputes between people about non-criminal matters.

House of Lords
Hears appeals from the Court of Session.

Court of Session
Outer House
Hears cases involving large sums of money e.g. damages, divorce.
Inner House
Hears appeals from Sheriff Court and Outer House.

Sheriff Courts
Hears majority of civil cases e.g. small money claims, divorce, eviction, bankruptcy, licensing.

Scottish Land Court
Settles disputes in agriculture and crofting.
Tribunals
Settling employment, immigration, child welfare, property, etc disputes.

Quick Test

1. What is the role of the Procurator Fiscal?
2. What is summary procedure and in which Scottish Courts would you find this procedure?
3. What is solemn procedure and in which Scottish Courts would you find this procedure?
4. Describe the court system in Scotland.

Sentencing

A person found guilty of a crime in Scotland can be given a **custodial sentence** of detention in a prison or Young Offenders Institution, or a **non-custodial sentence** served in the community.

Types of Non-Custodial Sentences

Fine	Offenders are sentenced to pay money as a deterrent to re-offending and sometimes compensation to victim. Amount depends on the seriousness of the offence and can be paid by instalments.
Fixed Penalty Notice (FPN)	On-the-spot fines are issued by police for low level anti-social behaviour like littering, drunkenness and vandalism and traffic wardens issue FPNs for parking offences. Aim is to release court time to deal with more serious offences.
Supervised Attendance Order (SAO)	Alternative to prison for people who fail to pay a fine. 'Pay' part of the fine with constructive activity like community service and/or education and financial management.
Probation	Supervision for six months to three years combined with action like alcohol and drug treatment to tackle the causes of offending.
Community Service Order (CSO)	Requirement to carry out up to 300 hours of unpaid work in the community helping elderly or disabled or working on environmental projects.
Restriction of Liberty Order (RLO) (electronic tagging)	Offender is placed on a curfew and restricted to named place (usually their home) for 12 hours a day for up to a year. They can also be excluded from certain places (like victims' homes) for up to a year. Offender wears a transmitter (electronic tag) on their ankle or wrist that alerts a control room if the offender is outside the permitted zones.
Drug Treatment and Testing Order (DTTO)	Drug treatment, random drug testing and regular court reviews to monitor withdrawal. 70% of crimes have a drug element and aim is reduce use and related crime like stealing to pay for drug habit.
Community Reparation Order (CRO)	Offender completes up to 100 hours of unpaid work in the local community for offences like graffiti or vandalism. Police and community councils have a say in what kind of work.
Anti-Social Behaviour Order (ASBO)	Covers street problems like rowdy behaviour, nuisance neighbours, damage to the environment like littering, vandalism and graffiti and bans someone from continuing with the behaviour, spending time with particular groups or visiting certain areas. Breaking an ASBO can mean a fine or up to five years in prison.

Proposed Changes

The **Scottish Prisons Commission** wants to move to **more non-custodial community sentencing** by ending prison sentences of less than six months and introducing:

- supervised bail orders reducing number of people in jail before trial
- conditional sentences with prison for not meeting conditions
- progress courts reviewing people on community sentences.

Arguments For and Against Community Sentences

Arguments for non-custodial community sentences	Arguments against non-custodial community sentences
More appropriate than prison for some types of offences where the offender poses no harm to the community. Prison is not effective in **rehabilitating** offenders (does not break the cycle of crime and punishment). Overcrowding and short sentences results in 'revolving door' – 62% those released re-offend within two years.	Prison is more appropriate for serious offences where the offender poses a danger to the community. **Combined structure** of custody, addressing offending behaviour with education and training and licensed early release into the community means prison can **rehabilitate** other offenders in controlled environment.
Break re-offending cycle by dealing with causes of crime and therefore more cost effective than prison. **Restorative justice** – offender addresses consequences of their behaviour on themselves, victims and the community. Still punishment because offenders take responsibility for their actions and work to rehabilitate (change their behaviour) and/or **compensate** (give something back to) the community.	Non-custodial sentences seen as a 'soft' option and denial of liberty as 'real' punishment. Crime cannot be committed while people are locked up, but non-custodial sentences are easy to break and not a **deterrent** to crime because not enough money is spent on effective rehabilitation programmes. 88% of those on DDTOs and 71% of RLOs (tagged) reoffend within two years.

Top Tip

Some people think non-custodial sentences are 'too soft'. Be prepared to discuss this

Quick Test

1. What is the difference between a **custodial** and a **non-custodial** sentence?

2. What are the main types of non-custodial sentences that a Scottish Court can give?

3. What changes have been proposed to sentencing in Scotland?

4. Explain the main arguments for and against non-custodial sentences.

Scottish Juvenile Justice System

In Scotland, children under 16 only appear in criminal court for serious offences like murder. Cases involving juveniles are dealt with by a **Children's Hearing**.

Children's Hearing System

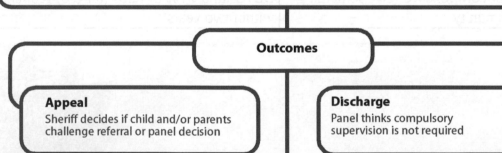

Referral
Police, social work, education or member of public contact **Children's Reporter** with concerns that child is victim of crime, has committed a crime, is not attending school, or is not being looked after properly.

Investigation
Reporter gets social work, police, school and medical reports and makes decision about how to proceed in best interests of the child.

Advice and/or **police warning**

Voluntary programme to work on problems

Hearing (Panel Meeting)
Reporter, three panel members (both male and female volunteers trained to work with families), child, parents or guardian, experts like social worker, teacher, educational psychologist, health visitor and child's representative (friend, relative or solicitor) or Safeguarder (someone appointed to look after the interests of the child). Hearing is not like a court. Discussion is around a table in private and the decision is reached in public.

Outcomes

Appeal
Sheriff decides if child and/or parents challenge referral or panel decision

Discharge
Panel thinks compulsory supervision is not required

Supervision requirement
Plan of work to support the child which may include placing the child in children's home, residential school or other secure accommodation, placing child with foster parents or keeping child with parents under supervision of social worker. Reviewed regularly and adapted as child's needs change.

Top Tip
Make sure you know what the Children's Panel can do to help young people with problems.

Proposals for Change

The **Scottish Prisons Commission** has recommended **Youth Hearings** for 16 and 17 year olds.

Arguments For and Against Hearing System

Arguments for Hearing System	Arguments against Hearing System
Keeps children and young people out of the adult court system. Care and protection, rather than punishment. Can work with young people before it reaches criminal stage.	Rapid turnover of panel members and limited number of outcomes. Too 'soft', not a real deterrent. 60% of referrals are care and protection and better dealt with elsewhere.
Supervision programmes to address behaviour combined with measures to deal with family, educational, psychological, drug, alcohol and other problems.	Set up 30 years ago when society was very different. Disintegration of families makes co-operation difficult and often problems getting children and families to comply.

Anti-Social Behaviour

Gangs of noisy or violent youths intimidate other people who do not feel safe to go out. The majority of public disorder incidents involve youths causing a 'nuisance' and if unchecked can often lead to more serious offences.

The **Anti-Social Behaviour Act, 2004** addresses this kind of behaviour by extending **Anti-Social Behaviour Orders (ASBOs)** to 12 to 15 year olds:

- allowing electronic tagging of under 16
- banning sale of spray paint to youths
- allowing the issue of parenting orders requiring parents to do more to control their children
- and giving the police powers to break up and disperse gangs of young people in areas where there has been serious anti-social behaviour.

However, some people argue that young people simply congregate elsewhere and that more services, like youth clubs, need to be provided for young people.

Quick Test

1. What actions can the Children's Panel take to support a young person?
2. Give the main arguments for and against the Children's Hearing system.
3. In what ways does the **Anti-Social Behaviour Act** apply to young people?
4. Explain how the Children's Hearing system deals with problems faced by some young people.

The Republic of South Africa

Background

South Africa is a large country with a population of over 48.6 million people in 2008. Its four main ethnic groups – Africans (Black indigenous people), Coloureds (people of mixed race), Whites (people of European descent), Indians and other Asians – have come about largely from its **colonial past** when Europeans owned the land.

South Africa is divided into nine large areas called **provinces**. The largest is the **Northern Cape** which is **rich in natural minerals**, such as diamonds and copper. The smallest is **Gauteng** which is **highly industrialised** and produces much of South Africa's wealth. South Africa relies heavily on **foreign investment** to strengthen its economy, and foreign debt, at **$39.71 billion,** is not as high as in other emerging nations. South Africa produces a huge range of raw materials that are demanded by other countries. This means that the economy has strengthened since the end of Apartheid, and the end of the economic sanctions that were placed on South Africa during this time.

Breakdown of the South African population

- Indian/Asian
- Coloured
- White
- African

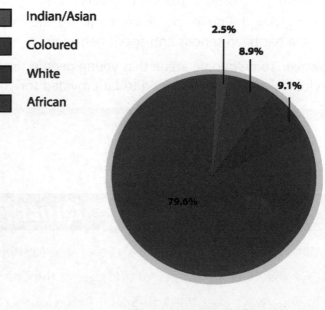

2.5%
8.9%
9.1%
79.6%

Source: *www.SouthAfrica.info, 2007*

Apartheid

South Africa has a troubled past which is largely due to its former political system of **Apartheid** ('separate development') put in place by the ruling white National Party in 1948 and finally removed in the early 1990s. Under Apartheid other racial groups were **marginalised** (given no power), and legally discriminated against, to the benefit of the Whites. For example, the **Mixed Marriages Act** outlawed marriages between Whites and non-Whites and the **Bantu Homelands Citizenship Act** created all-Black areas and gave Whites access to the best land and the best social and economic opportunities. The National Party held full political control over South Africa and political participation among non-Whites was stifled.

Nelson Mandela became the first Black President of South Africa in 1994

Apartheid, and its legacy, will be felt for generations but a great deal of social, political and economic improvement has been made. One of the main figures associated with the collapse of Apartheid is **Nelson Mandela**. He was also the first Black President of South Africa.

Top Tip

Apartheid will not be directly examined in the exam but you will have to understand it in order to gauge the progress that has been made in the last 20 years.

Quick Test

1. Describe the main population groups in South Africa.
2. How many provinces are there in South Africa?
3. Name the largest province in South Africa and describe some of its features.
4. Describe the main features of the former Apartheid system?

Social and Economic Inequalities

The majority of inequalities in South Africa have been caused by the **legacy of Apartheid**. However, other factors have also led to social and economic inequalities.

Top Tip
You will lose valuable marks if you discuss Apartheid as a current issue.

Education

Education in South Africa is compulsory for children aged between 7 and 15 but it is not free. A **two-tier system** exists which favours the wealthy because poorer parents, particularly those with a large number of children, find it impossible to pay school fees. Many children from the poorest families only complete primary education and are trapped in poverty because without a good education they cannot compete for jobs that will improve their living standards.

Employment

Blacks, Coloureds and Indians/Asians make up approximately 80% of the workforce, yet they represent only a tiny proportion of those in the highest paid professions. This is improving but not fast enough considering these ethnic groups account for 91% of the population.

Unemployment

Unemployment is a real area of concern in South Africa, not just because of the impact on the national and global economy, but also because of the impact on the lives of individuals. South Africa has **no welfare state** so there is no 'safety net' for those who cannot earn an income.

Government figures quote the unemployment range at 20 to 25%, but the true level is more like **40%** – almost half of the workforce. However, the figures for Blacks are much higher.

Housing

As a direct result of Apartheid many people are still living in poor quality housing in townships, like Soweto in Johannesburg. Although one million new houses were built between 1994 and 2004 this has not met the massive **housing shortfall**.

Health

HIV/AIDS is one of the greatest areas of concern. Several high profile South African political figures, like Nelson Mandela and Chief Buthelezi, the leader of the Inkatha Freedom Party, have lost family members to AIDS.

The government of Thabo Mbeki has been criticised because it refused to accept the link between HIV and AIDS and did not provide sufficient sex education programmes for school pupils. The **Constitutional Court** has intervened to force the government to provide expensive drugs which block the action of the HIV retro-virus.

Other ongoing health problems include **malnutrition** and problems associated with poverty and lack of access to health care – this is shocking when we consider the wealth of South Africa.

Crime

Massive wealth inequalities in South Africa have led to **high levels** of violent crime and theft, impacting all racial groups. High levels of unemployment, disconnection from the community, poverty and resentment all contribute to South Africa having one of the highest murder rates in the world. This has resulted in a climate of fear. Money can buy wealthier citizens protection because they are able to live in 'gated' communities with security guards. However, for the people of the townships, like Soweto, private security guards are very far from the reality of day-to-day life. Despite attempts by the police to take action, in these areas 'rough justice' exists – people from the community punish those who break the law.

High levels of crime coupled with negative media attention have served to stop some travellers from considering South Africa as a holiday destination – this impacts on the economy.

Top Tip

It is important to remember that social and economic issues are interrelated.

Quick Test

1. Explain why crime is a problem in South Africa?
2. Explain why education is still an issue of concern in South Africa?
3. Describe the health problems that still exist in South Africa.
4. Explain why unemployment continues to be a problem in South Africa.

Government Policies

Reconstruction and Development Programme (RDP)

RDP was an very **ambitious** group of policies aimed at creating racial equality by improving the living standards of those who suffered as a result of Apartheid, but there were a number of **problems**. The most apparent of these was that the **targets were too ambitious** to achieve in a short time. For example, RDP aimed to build one million new homes within **five** years, but this actually took **ten** years to achieve and did not provide enough housing for those in need.

Growth, Employment and Redistribution (GEAR)

GEAR replaced RDP with the aim of **strengthening the economy** so that the government could better provide for the population by helping them help themselves. The focus on the economy encouraged growth that had **stagnated** during the Apartheid years.

Black entrepreneurship and movement into professional occupations was encouraged so that the Black population would be **better represented** in business and the highest skilled and paid professions.

Some government tactics were unpopular because of the sale of national utilities such as electricity and gas, but in the short term this gave the government money to improve services. However, long term the government have lost control meaning that private companies are free to charge what they want.

Top Tip
Use the internet to regularly update your knowledge of current policies.

Affirmative Action

Affirmative Action (positive discrimination) aims to ensure that all ethnic groups have a **fair** share of the country's wealth and opportunities. It uses positive discrimination to redress inequalities and create a more equal society.

Many South Africans now feel that this practice should be stopped because it is **unconstitutional**, but the government still uses Affirmative Action to create a diverse workforce. For example, under the **Employment Equity Act** companies have to **discriminate in favour** of the Black majority as well as minorities like the disabled. A company with **over 50 employees** must reflect the make-up of the population or they can be fined.

Black Economic Empowerment (BEE)

BEE was implemented recently to ensure that the spirit of **Black economic entrepreneurship** was supported by the government and private business. It was also implemented to make sure that Non-Whites have a share of power that reflects their majority. All companies now have a responsibility to provide skills and training for Blacks in promoted posts.

Increasing numbers of Black South Africans have well-paid jobs in business

Top Tip

Make sure you know about at least **three** policies, in detail.

Quick Test

1. For what reasons was RDP replaced by GEAR?
2. Describe the measures the South African government introduced to tackle the distribution of wealth?
3. Explain what is meant by Affirmative Action and give an example of an Affirmative Action policy.
4. Describe two policies the South African government has put in place to address social and economic inequality.

Successes and Limitations of Government Policies

Education

All children have the right to be educated and all children get one free nutritional meal a day – the **Mandela Sandwich** – which has gone some way to tackling malnutrition and ill health. As a result of improved nutrition and health, examination passes have increased.

Higher education in South African is vibrant, with many universities producing well-educated people of all races who will drive the economy forward. However, many initial targets have not been met and there are still gaps in basic education. It is not free and the poorest cannot afford for their children to be educated to the age of 15.

Unemployment and Employment

Although education is not equally accessed by all, Black, Coloured and Indian/Asian professionals have emerged. With continued educational improvements more will emerge. The 2010 Football World Cup in South Africa will boost the economy and tourism. However, unemployment remains a **major** problem because of a **'lost generation'** of Black South Africans who received very little, or no, education during Apartheid.

Black, Coloured and Indian/Asian South Africans have higher levels of unemployment and lower pay than White South Africans and the Employment Equity Act and the Black Economic Empowerment Act have not entirely dealt with the problem.

Health

Healthcare projects have expanded into rural areas. South African children under six and pregnant women have access to **free** healthcare which has improved **mortality** and **morbidity rates**. However, there are still significant inequalities and life expectancy has dropped to approximately **50 years** of age.

Many young professionals have lost their lives to HIV/AIDS, and many children have lost parents, creating a weakness in the economy. This may improve after the Constitutional Court ruling that the South African Government has to invest in anti-retro viral drugs for HIV/AIDS sufferers.

Housing

The one million new homes promised by the South African Government were eventually delivered, resulting in a substantial increase in the living standards of many South Africans. Many people are benefiting from access to **sanitation** and **electricity**. However, electricity is provided by private utility companies that can charge as they wish. Electricity is available but many people **cannot afford** it.

Redistribution of land is a significant problem because land transfer back into the hands of Black South Africans has been slow – a fact recognised by the South African Government. The government have aimed to restore ownership of land to those forced off their land during white rule, and give the poor and disadvantaged land to work. Although many **hectares** of land have been redistributed it is not enough to fulfil government targets.

At present, only **3%** of agricultural land previously owned by whites has been transferred – the government target is **30%** by 2015. This may be due to the resistance of White farmers who feel that the land they farm is rightfully theirs, the difficulty in proving land claims and the high compensation costs involved.

Crime

More Black South Africans are being recruited into the police force. It is hoped they will act as role models for the young and impoverished who may otherwise turn to crime. However, violent crime is still a **major** problem – between April 2007 and March 2008 the **South African Police Service (SAPS)** registered 18,487 murders.

Many ordinary people are frightened, while those with a high standard of living feel more secure with **private security** and **gated** communities.

Top Tip
Evaluate the success of each policy by examining the targets set and the extent of progress made.

Quick Test

1. In what ways has the South African Government tried to improve the lives of the poorest people?
2. For what reasons is HIV/AIDS still a major problem for South Africa?
3. Explain why land redistribution has been slow.
4. How successfully has the South African Government tackled inequalities in health and education?

South African Government Structure

South Africa has been a **constitutional democracy** since 1994. The rights and responsibilities of South African politicians and citizens are outlined in a document called **the constitution** which guarantees liberty and equality for all citizens – rights that did not exist under Apartheid.

"Every person shall have the right to equality before the law and to equal protection of the law ... No person shall be unfairly discriminated against, directly or indirectly ..."

South African Constitution

There are **three** levels of government in South Africa; **national, provincial** and **local**. The constitution ensures that these levels of government are separate and that they have to co-operate.

National Government

Laws (legislation) relating to the whole country are made by the National Parliament in Cape Town. The National Parliament is **bicameral**; this means there are two Houses – the **National Assembly** and the **National Council of Provinces**.

The **National Assembly** has **400** Members of Parliament and is elected every five years using a system of Proportional Representation (PR).

The **National Council of Provinces** has **90** Representatives – ten from each of the nine provinces – who oversee the work of the National Government that relates to provincial and local government.

To pass bills, the two Houses of the South African Parliament must work together to make sure legislation benefits the people of South Africa.

The **Constitutional Court**, with its eleven politically neutral judges, makes sure that proposed legislation **does not break** the rules of the South African Constitution.

Former President Thabo Mbeki

Top Tip
The constitution of South Africa can be changed, but it requires a **two thirds majority** in both Houses.

The head of the National Government is the **President**. The President can serve a maximum of **two terms** (a total of 10 years).

There is a limit to the Presidential term so that no one person becomes too powerful. This is one of many **safeguards** to democracy that was written into the South African Constitution to protect against the abuse of power that existed during Apartheid.

The President is elected by the members of the National Assembly. The ANC is the ruling party in South Africa; therefore, it is likely that the President will be the leader of the ANC. The President appoints a group of Ministers and a Depute President to take leading roles in areas such as health and education. The name given to this appointed group of people is the **Cabinet**.

Provincial Government

Each of the nine provinces has its own provincial government headed by a **Premier**. Each has between **30-80 representatives** – depending on the population of the province – who are elected every five years. The Premier also serves a **maximum** of two five year terms and appoints an Executive Council that acts as a Provincial Cabinet.

Local Government

South Africa is divided into local municipalities, or councils, made up of elected representatives who put policies in place that specifically benefit their local area. Municipal councils are responsible for a range of **local services**, such as the delivery of electricity, water, sewage and sanitation provision and roads. They may also undertake tasks delegated to them by National or Provincial Government. The head of each council is a **Mayor**, elected by the council.

Quick Test

1. Name the two Houses that make up the South African Parliament.
2. How many MPs are there in the National Assembly?
3. Explain why the President and Premier are only allowed to serve two terms.
4. Describe the role of the Constitutional Court.

National and Provincial Election Results

The first **non-race** based elections took place in South Africa in 1994; since then all South African governments have been dominated by the **African National Congress (ANC).** Many people claim that South Africa is a **one party state** because although elections are no longer race based, traditional party support still is. The ANC draw most of their support from the Black majority population – many of whom see the ANC as the party who conquered Apartheid. However, there are a huge number of political parties who participate in elections – some would suggest that there are **too many** to provide a real, strong alternative to the ANC.

Despite a growing number of South Africans being dissatisfied with the speed of social and economic progress, the ANC still dominates the **municipal elections**. In the 2006 election the ANC won 66.3% of the vote; only slightly down on their most recent performance in the 2004 National Assembly election.

Top Tip
When looking at a country's election results over a number of years try to spot patterns and trends.

2004

National Assembly

Political Party	Percentage of the vote	Number of Assembly Seats
African National Congress	69.7%	279
Democratic Alliance	12.4%	50
Inkatha Freedom Party	7.0%	28
Nine other parties	10.9%	43
Electoral Turnout	*76.7%*	

2004 saw a **decline** in electoral turnout, revealing dissatisfaction with the ANC's solutions to social and economic problems. However, along with this decline in turnout, the ANC **increased** their share of the vote to a two-thirds majority in the National Assembly.

Provincial Elections

In 2004 the ANC won control of **almost all** the nine provinces emphasising the control they hold over the politics of South Africa. In the remaining provinces they share power with the **Democratic Alliance** and the **Inkatha Freedom Party**. In the provinces the ANC did not win they still gained between **45-48%** of the vote.

These national and provincial results therefore deepened and strengthened the position the ANC established in all elections since 1994.

1999

National Assembly

Political Party	Percentage of the Vote	Number of Assembly Seats
African National Congress	66.4%	266
Democratic Party	9.6%	38
Inkatha Freedom Party	8.6%	34
Ten Other Parties	15.4%	62
Electoral Turnout	*89.3%*	

Provincial Elections

In 1999 the ANC won control of seven of the nine provinces. In the Western Cape the ANC shared power with The New National Party and in KwaZulu Natal they shared power with the Inkatha Freedom Party.

Dominance of the ANC

National Assembly Elections

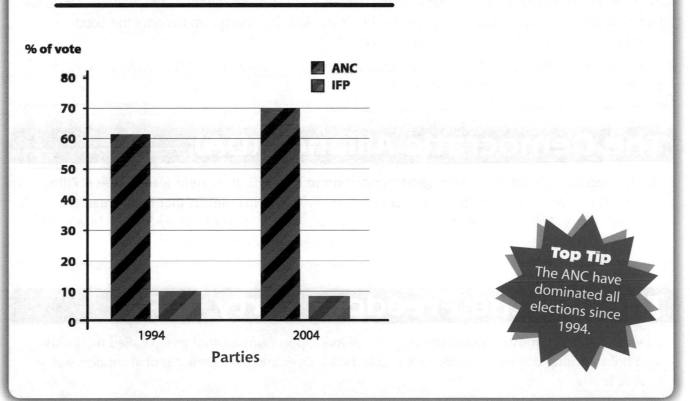

% of vote

Top Tip
The ANC have dominated all elections since 1994.

Quick Test

1. What evidence is there that the ANC has wide support in South Africa?

2. Explain why the ANC is so dominant in elections in South Africa.

3. For what reasons was there a decline in turnout in 2004?

4. Give reasons to support and oppose the view that South Africa is 'healthy democracy'.

South African Political Parties

Multi-party democracy

There are a large number of political parties in South Africa. This system of **multi-party democracy** means that the South African electorate have a great deal of **choice**. However, the drawback is that having so many political parties may split their support and no real opposition will emerge. At the moment, the ANC dominates politics in South Africa – leading some to believe that the country is a **one party state**. However, a more consistent opposition now seems to be emerging.

The African National Congress (ANC)

The ANC are the **party of government** in South Africa and draw their support mainly from the majority Black population. However, there have been some changes. In 2005 the National Party disbanded and many of its former members '**crossed the floor**' to join the ANC.

In 2008, the President of South Africa, Thabo Mbeki, was forced to resign by the National Executive Committee of the ANC. Jacob Zuma, the leader of the ANC is expected to become the South African President if the ANC win the 2009 election.

One major problem facing the ANC is internal divisions – it is thought that this could be a major challenge to the party in forthcoming years.

The Democratic Alliance (DA)

The Democratic Alliance is the **strongest opposition** to the ANC. Its current leader, **Helen Zille**, took power in 2007. The DA fought the last two elections with manifestos that highlighted the weakness of the ANC in delivering its promises – an area which concerns many South Africans. They also stated in their manifesto that they aim to be a non-racial alternative to the ANC.

The Inkatha Freedom Party (IFP)

The Inkatha Freedom Party draws the majority of its support from a tribal group called the **Zulus**, who hold a strong degree of power in KwaZulu Natal. Over the years their national support has declined.

The leader of the IFP is **Chief Buthelezi**. One of the IFP's goals is to see more power sharing between the **spheres** of government – National, Provincial and Municipal. If this were to happen the IFP would probably gain an even more significant share of power in KwaZulu Natal and areas with a high concentration of Zulus.

The (New) National Party (NP)

The National Party were the party of Apartheid. However, **F.W de Klerk**, who was the leader of the NP in the 1990s, worked with **Nelson Mandela** to remove the oppressive Apartheid system and introduce non-race based politics.

After numerous reinventions, in-fighting and falling popular support the NP disbanded in 2005. Many members joined the ANC and other political parties.

Pressure Groups

One of the best known pressure groups in South Africa is the **Congress of South African Trade Unions, COSATU**. This group campaigned during Apartheid, and in subsequent years, for a democratic, discrimination free South Africa.

Despite being a trade union COSATU shares a close relationship with the ANC, raising the question – can a pressure group represent the people if it is so closely **affiliated** with the party of government?

Top Tip

Although the Democratic Alliance forms the main opposition to the ANC, it does not have significant enough support to threaten their power.

Quick Test

1. What evidence is there that South Africa is a one-party state?
2. Name three political parties in South Africa and describe what they aim to achieve.
3. Name a South African pressure group and describe the cause it fights for.
4. Describe the political opposition faced by the South African Government.

Economic Development and Change

China is the largest country in Asia and has a population of over 1.3 billion. It is a **communist** country which has undergone massive economic and social change in recent years which has resulted in growing inequalities.

Market Economy

China has changed the way it runs its economy. Private companies have replaced **State Owned Enterprises (SOEs)**, and now produce 70% of output. The market economy has grown rapidly – Gross Domestic Product (GDP) and Personal Disposable Income (PDI) have more than trebled in ten years.

Foreign Trade and Investment

Cheap labour and tax incentives encouraged foreign businesses to set up in coastal **Special Enterprise Zones (SEZs)** assembling goods, mostly for export. China then developed into a producer of high-quality manufactured goods for the growing home market and for export.

Foreign trade doubled after China joined the **World Trade Organisation (WTO)** in 2001 and Chinese companies now invest abroad. **Nanking Automobiles** bought MG Rover in 2007 which gave them access to Western technology and markets.

Top Tip
China has moved from state control to a market economy.

Agriculture

The **Household Responsibility System** replaced state control. Farmers can lease land, grow their own crops and sell any surplus from state quotas. In rural areas **Township and Village Enterprises (TVEs)** provide non-agricultural jobs and raise income.

Migration

China changed its *hukou* (population registration) system to allow rural residents to move to jobs in urban areas and register for education and health services.

Westernisation

China has an increasingly Westernised lifestyle. Rising income creates a demand for Western fashion, cars and fast foods, as well as movies and sport on satellite TV. In 2008, China had over 600 McDonalds and 2000 KFCs. Between 2004 and 2008, internet use has doubled, new car registrations have trebled and 80% of people in urban areas own their own homes.

However, not all parts of China have benefited from these changes. There is inequality between rural and urban areas and a widening gap between rich and poor.

Regional differences in China- Comparison of Gansu and Guangdong

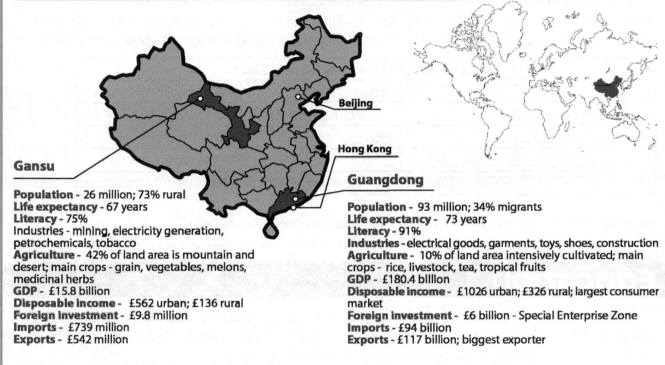

Beijing

Hong Kong

Gansu

Population - 26 million; 73% rural
Life expectancy - 67 years
Literacy - 75%
Industries - mining, electricity generation, petrochemicals, tobacco
Agriculture - 42% of land area is mountain and desert; main crops - grain, vegetables, melons, medicinal herbs
GDP - £15.8 billion
Disposable income - £562 urban; £136 rural
Foreign investment - £9.8 million
Imports - £739 million
Exports - £542 million

Guangdong

Population - 93 million; 34% migrants
Life expectancy - 73 years
Literacy - 91%
Industries - electrical goods, garments, toys, shoes, construction
Agriculture - 10% of land area intensively cultivated; main crops - rice, livestock, tea, tropical fruits
GDP - £180.4 billion
Disposable income - £1026 urban; £326 rural; largest consumer market
Foreign investment - £6 billion - Special Enterprise Zone
Imports - £94 billion
Exports - £117 billion; biggest exporter

Source: *China Statistical Yearbook and China.org (Adapted) – figures refer to 2006*

Quick Test

1. Describe the way in which China has changed the way it runs its economy.

2. Explain how the following have helped to develop China's economy: SEZs, agricultural reforms and changes to *hukou* system?

3. In what ways has the lifestyle of many Chinese become more Westernised?

4. What **conclusions** can be drawn about the differences between the richest and poorest province in China?

Social and Economic Inequalities

Wealth

Wealth in China is **unevenly distributed**. Half the population earn 2000 Yuan (£140) a year, while the top 4% of the population earn ten times that amount. There is also a **big difference between rural and urban areas**. The average urban income is three times the rural income and migrant workers from the countryside earn even less. In 2007, the average annual income of an unskilled migrant worker was 1200 Yuan (£84) compared with the national average of 9600 Yuan (£660).

China – Rural/Urban inequalities, 2007		
	Urban	**Rural**
PDI* per head per year	13,786 Yuan (£1010)	4140 Yuan (£303)
Unemployment rate	4%	17% (estimated)
% of population with no education	2.5%	8.7%
*PDI = Personal Disposable Income – amount people have to spend		

Source: US-China Business Council, CIA Factbook, UN Development Programme (Adapted)

Education

Chinese children are supposed to have **nine years of free compulsory education** but the system is unequal. Children in rural areas often drop out to boost the family income. Only 1.5% of children in Tibet receive secondary education compared with 60% in Beijing.

Local authorities charge fees for books, and other expenses, which poorer families cannot afford. If migrant workers do not have an urban *hukou* they have to pay more.

The 2003 **Law on Promotion of Private Education** allows many better off Chinese people send their children to private schools, or abroad, to be educated.

Health

Under the old system, the *danwei* (work unit) provided health coverage, but now half of the urban population, and 90% of the rural population, have no medical coverage from employers. The better-off can afford private medical insurance.

There is also **considerable corruption in the system**. Half the money for doctors' salaries comes from drug sales, leading to over-prescribing and unnecessary procedures.

Employment and Unemployment

The end of the state system, and the **'Iron Rice Bowl'** of a guaranteed job for life, means those without the skills necessary for the private sector have fallen behind. 43 million jobs have been lost from State Owned Enterprises, but only 16.5 million created by private sector.

Housing

End of the *danwei* means less subsidised state housing. The better-off can afford to buy houses and the **Property Law of 2007** legalises the buying and selling of property. However, **the less well-off cannot afford house prices**, which are rising by 25% a year in some areas.

The construction boom has also lead to **urban sprawl and pollution**, as well as protests against some developments.

Top Tip
China is becoming a more unequal society.

Crime

In the last 20 years, **crime in China has grown even faster than the economy**. Crimes such as theft, drug use, internet fraud, prostitution and gambling show the change from the former strictly run Chinese society.

School drop-out rate and large numbers of migrant workers leaving children in the care of relatives are blamed for the fact that two-thirds of the criminal cases involve juveniles.

'**Mafia capitalism**' involving organised gangs (triads) in crimes like counterfeiting, people trafficking, smuggling and money laundering has created a huge hidden economy.

20% of China's consumer goods are counterfeit and China's business reputation and standing in the world is threatened by **corruption** among officials.

Quick Test

1. What evidence is there of an unequal distribution of wealth in China?
2. What inequalities have resulted because of the end of the *danwei* and the **'Iron Rice Bowl'**?
3. Why is crime threatening China's reputation?
4. Describe the inequalities which exist between rural and urban areas in China.

Government Responses

The 11th Five Year Plan

The Chinese Government wants to continue rapid economic development, but it is aware of growing inequalities and its **11th Five Year Plan** has measures to tackle these.

TARGETS OF THE 11TH FIVE YEAR PLAN, 2005 – 2010
Average Urban PDI* per head per year to rise by 30% to 13,390 yuan (£975)
Average Rural PDI* per head per year to rise by 30% to 4,150 yuan (£302)
Average number of school years to rise by 0.5 to 9 years
People in urban areas covered by basic pension to rise by 49 million to 223 million
Number covered by New Rural Co-operative Medical Care scheme to rise to >80%
Number of new jobs created to rise by 45 million
Number of farmers transferred to non-agricultural jobs to rise by 45 million

* PDI = Personal Disposable Income – amount people have to spend.

Source: *National Development and Reform Commission of PRC (Adapted)*

Wealth

The Chinese Government provides a **Minimum Living Allowance** of 15 Yuan (£1.10) a month in urban areas, and 10 Yuan (73p) in rural areas, to 58 million people on low incomes, 60% of whom are in rural areas. The Government has also tried to address the imbalance between rich and poor through **tax reforms**. The amount of income at which people start paying tax was raised in 2008 which means people on lower incomes will pay less tax. The very rich are taxed at 45% of their income and the Government is taking action to stop the rich avoiding tax.

Education

The **National Project of Compulsory Education in Impoverished Areas** provides finance to improve schooling in poor areas, including distance learning projects.

In 2007, the Chinese Government set up a fund to cover school fees in rural areas and scholarships are also available for higher education for poorer families.

The Government also subsidises eight million children in **boarding schools** in an attempt to cut the drop out rate and improve education in rural areas.

Top Tip
Use the internet regularly to update your knowledge of China.

Health

In 2002, the Government introduced the **New Rural Co-operative Medical Care System** which now covers 80% of the rural population. The annual cost of medical insurance under the system is 50 Yuan (£3.50) per person. The patient pays 10 Yuan (70p) and the Government and province share the rest of the cost. If a patient needs hospital treatment they have to pay 20% of the cost at a local clinic and 70% at a major hospital, but this is too expensive for many rural people.

In 2007, 79 cities piloted the **Healthy China 2020 Programme**. This will be extended to the whole country and will provide a basic universal health system similar to the UK National Health Service.

The Government has also acted against corruption. In 2007, the head of the State Food and Drugs Administration, **Zheng Xiaoyu,** was sentenced to death for taking bribes.

Employment and Unemployment

A '**Go West**' policy provides incentives for foreign companies like Microsoft, Nokia and Ford to set up in China's poorer Western provinces. However, this has only had limited success due to remoteness and poor transport. Trade from the Western provinces is still only 5% of the national total.

The Government set up **vocational schools** to develop skills for the new economy, but they are not popular. Employers prefer their own training and parents see them as a dead end and prefer general education for their children.

Tackling Corruption and Crime

The **Central Committee on Discipline Inspection (CCDI)** of the **Communist Party of China** (CPC) has set up rules, known as the '**Ten Taboos**', to ban bribery and other corrupt practices among officials. It has also set up a hotline and website for people to report corruption – several high ranking officials have been sacked or jailed. **Chen Liangyu**, former Communist Party chief in Shanghai, was jailed for 18 years in 2008 for accepting bribes and embezzling hundreds of millions of yuan from the city's pension fund.

The Government tackles crime in '**Strike Hard**' campaigns where they target particular crimes and give harsh sentences.

20% of all consumer goods in China are counterfeit and in 2008 the Government launched the '**Thunderstorm**' campaign to crack down on counterfeiters.

Quick Test

1. What measures has the Chinese Government introduced to tackle wealth inequalities?
2. Describe the ways in which the Chinese Government is tackling corruption and crime.
3. Explain how the Chinese Government tries to tackle inequalities between rural and urban areas?
4. Describe the measures the Chinese Government has introduced to improve health care.

Political Issues

Representation

China does not have Western-style representation where political parties compete and voters decide which policies they want put into practice. The views of only one party count – the **Communist Party of China (CPC)** – and the top leaders of the party also provide the Government. **Hu Jintao** is Chairman (head) of the CPC and President (head of state) of China. The membership of the CPC is unrepresentative – over three-quarters are over 35 and only 20% are women – but it still influences every aspect of life in China.

To join the CPC people have to be recommended by two party members, be thoroughly checked and tested by the local party and have a year of probation. Who you know is important to doing well in China, so party membership continues to increase – 13 million new members in the last ten years – because members get access to people who can advance their careers.

The CPC has local organisations throughout China and they send delegates every five years to the 2000-member **National Party** Congress which chooses a **Central Committee**. The main job of the Central Committee is to choose a **Politburo** of top party leaders who run the party and the country. It also chooses a **Discipline Commission** to deal with party members suspected of corruption, bad management or not following the party line.

The **Politburo** is a 24-member cabinet of the top people in the CPC, including party secretaries from big cities like Beijing and Shanghai and provinces like Guangdong, which sets policy.

The real power, however, lies with nine members of the **Standing Committee** of the CPC who hold the top posts in the CPC and the Government. Its members include President **Hu Jintao**, Premier (Prime Minister) **Wen Jiabao** and Chairman of the National People's Congress, **Wu Bangguo**.

National People's Congress

The **National People's Congress** is China's 'parliament' and is made up of 3000 delegates elected for five years by **local people's congresses** in the cities, provinces and armed forces. It only meets once a year and the real influence lies with the 150-member **Standing Committee** of the NPC which meets every two months. In theory, the Standing Committee has powers to make laws and change the constitution, but in reality 70% of the delegates, and all the senior office holders, are members of CPC, so it merely 'rubber stamps' decisions made by the leadership of the CPC.

The NPC also elects the President, Vice-President, members of the **State Council** and the chairman of the **Military Affairs Commission.** The Military Affairs Commission decides all matters to do with the **People's Liberation Army (PLA)** and the job of chairman usually goes to the most powerful figure in the party who becomes commander-in-chief.

State Council

The 50-member State Council, composed of the premier, vice-premiers, state councillors and heads of ministries, makes sure party policy gets implemented and maintains law and order. It draws up and manages the national economic plan and budget. In theory, it is accountable to the NPC, but in practice the State Council draws up legislation which the NPC approves. The full council meets once a month, but the more important **Standing Committee** of the State Council meets twice a week.

China – Political Structure

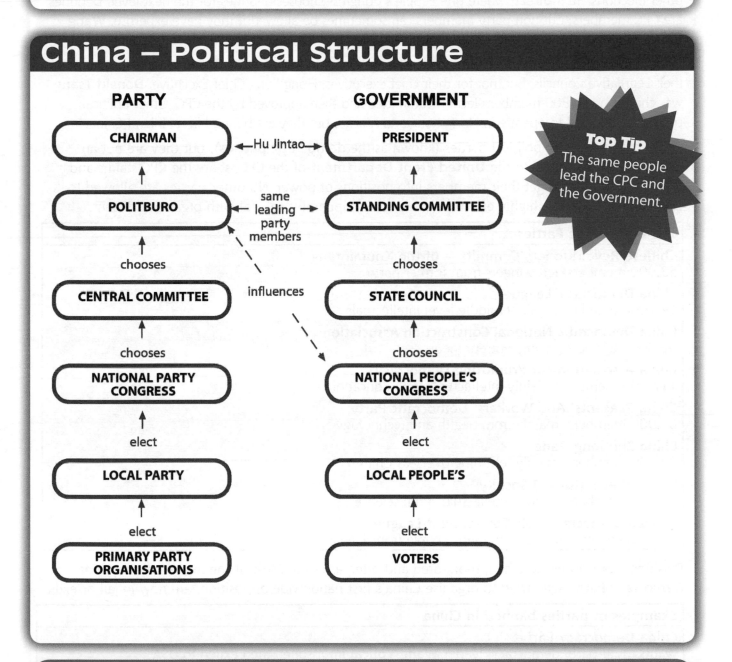

Top Tip
The same people lead the CPC and the Government.

Quick Test

1. Describe the stages a member of CPC would go through from applying for membership to reaching the top of the party.
2. Explain how the CPC and the Chinese Government are linked?
3. What is the role of the National People's Congress in the Government of China?
4. Describe the opportunities for political representation in China.

Participation

Elections and Political Parties

The Chinese Constitution gives people over 18 the right to vote, but opportunities to do so are limited. **Direct elections** only take place at local level for village committees and local People's Congresses. All other elections are **indirect**, where one People's Congress chooses deputies for the next level. Deputies are CPC members, but non-party members can sometimes be allowed if they have expertise. **Wang Gang**, Minister of Science and Technology, is first the non-CPC member to reach State Council level.

Under the **one country-two systems** policy, Hong Kong and Macao have direct elections for part of their Legislative Councils, but, not for their chief executives. Hong Kong Chief Executive, **Donald Tsang**, was chosen by an 800-member election committee and then approved by the CPC. Other political parties are allowed to operate in Hong Kong and Macao, but they are banned in mainland China.

China has eight other political parties (known as the **democratic parties**), but they are not an opposition. They report to the **United Front Department** of the CPC, share the CPC's aims and rely on its support to get their members into positions of power. No other parties are allowed to operate and there is a highly effective state security apparatus to deal with organised dissent.

The Democratic Parties
Chinese Revolutionary Committee of the Koumintang   53,000 members; left wingers from former party
China Democratic League   144,000 members; mainly middle level intellectuals
China Democratic National Construction Association   50,000 members; mainly entrepreneurs
China Association For Promoting Democracy   117,500 members; mainly intellectuals from education
China Peasants' And Workers' Democratic Party   65,000 members; mainly from health and technology
China Zhi Gong Dang   10,000 members; mainly returning overseas Chinese
September 3 (Juisan) Society   68,000 members; mainly intellectuals from science
Taiwan Democratic Self-Government League   1,600 members; mainly prominent people from Taiwan

Dissidents are closely watched, monitored and often arrested. Most of the leaders of the **China Democracy Party**, who tried to organise China's first nationwide opposition, are now in jail or exile.

Examples of parties banned in China
China Democracy Party   Wants multi-party democracy; leader **Wang Youcai** imprisoned then exiled to USA
Green Watch   Monitors environmental abuses; leader **Tan Kai** imprisoned for "illegally obtaining state secrets"
National Democratic Party of Tibet   Wants independence for Tibet; supports Dalai Lama
Southern Mongolian Democratic Alliance   Wants independence for Inner Mongolia; leader **Hada** imprisoned for "spying"
East Turkistan (Xinjiang) National Congress   Wants independence of Xinjiang; branded "terrorist organisation" by China

Provinces and Cities

Power and decisions flow down from the top and participation at local level is only allowed if it does not threaten central control. Some provinces, like Tibet, Xinjian and Inner Mongolia, want more independence, but this has been repressed. Rich provinces, like Guangdong and Fujian and cities like Shanghai, are allowed to run their own economic affairs and can build up local power bases. The Chinese Government relies on their tax revenues and their leaders have powerful positions in party. **Wang Yang**, party chief of richest province, Guangdong and **Yu Zhengsheng**, party chief of richest city, Shanghai are members of Politburo.

Top Tip
Opportunities for participation are limited in China.

Emerging Middle Class

An increasing number of wealthy non-party members are in contact with the West and see how Western business people influence Governments. It is possible that the growing Chinese middle class may want more participation.

Outside Influences

in July 2008, there were 250 million internet users in China (more than in the USA) and an increasing number of satellite TVs. The Government is finding it more difficult to stop access to information that might undermine the **party line**. However, there is little call for the overthrow of the CPC and rapid introduction of a western-style democracy.

Divisions in the CPC

There are divisions within the CPC about how to allow the people to participate in politics without ending the one-party system. One view is to continue rapid development and allow more participation at local level. The opposite view wants to retain strong central control to tackle inequalities and keep the country together.

Hu Jintao named two possible successors at the 2007 17th Communist Party Congress. The Shanghai Party Secretary **Xi Jinping** and Liaoning Party Secretary, **Li Keqiang**. Xi Jinping is the son of a high ranking Chinese official, has experience in rich coastal areas and is the choice of the entrepreneurs and the emerging middle class. Li Keqiang is the son of a low ranking official, worked his way up and has experience in the poorer interior provinces. These two represent the different views and will be competing within the party to become the next Chinese president.

Quick Test

1. What opportunities are there for people to participate in elections in China?
2. Describe the conditions under which political parties are allowed to operate in China.
3. Explain why changes in the Chinese economy and lifestyle might bring demands for more participation.
4. Describe ways in which participation is limited in China.

Human Rights

Freedom of Expression

The media in China is censored. People can be arrested for criticising the Government or praising multi-party democracy. The **Law on Guarding State Secrets** has a 'catch-all' clause of 'any other secrets' that is used to stop criticism. In 2008 China introduced **Open Government Information (OGI) Regulations** but they do not give the public a 'right to know'. The **'Great Firewall of China'** blocks internet websites of religious, dissident and opposition groups, as well as YouTube, Wikipedia and foreign news sites. Internet access is difficult to control and in 2008 the Chinese Government allowed access to English language BBC news sites.

The Chinese population is monitored by the **Hokou** and the **Dang'an** (a file containing details of a person's life from school onwards). **Public Security Bureau (PSB)** holds the Dang'an and employment, housing, pension, passport and right to have a child depend on favourable entries. The **State Subversion Law** covers everything from organising and scheming to acting to split the nation, riot or subvert the state. Police and troops are deployed to stop protests, as happened in **Tiananmen Square** in 1989. Some of the protest leaders are still in jail and **Ding Zilin**, leader of the **Tiananmen Mothers** who pressure the Chinese Government to acknowledge those killed, is still under 24-hour surveillance.

> *"Citizens of the People's Republic of China enjoy freedom of speech, of the press, of assembly, or association, of procession and of demonstration."*
>
> **Chinese Constitution—Article 35**

Top Tip
Rights in the Chinese Constitution are not always given in practice.

Religious Freedom

China officially recognises five religions – Buddhism, Taoism, Islam, Catholicism and Protestantism. They have to register with **State Administration for Religious Affairs (SARA)** and follow a state approved version. SARA considers some religions, like Buddhism in Tibet and Islam in Xinjiang, a particular threat.

Tibet was once an independent Buddhist country with the Dalai Lama as its spiritual leader. It has been under Chinese rule since 1951 and in 1959 the Dalai Lama fled into exile in India. Since then incentives have been offered to ethnic Chinese to move to Tibet and they now outnumber ethnic Tibetans 2 to 1. There is a repressive regime to stop opposition. The Tibetan flag is outlawed but despite this there have been several attempts at uprisings. Protests in Tibet, and worldwide, coincided with the 2008 Olympic torch relay for the Beijing games.

> *"Citizens of the People's Republic of China enjoy freedom of religious belief."*
>
> **Chinese Constitution—Article 36**

Xinjiang has a largely Muslim population but migration of ethnic Chinese is encouraged and they now form half the population. Only authorised mosques are allowed and public displays of religion are banned.

China has linked demands for more religious freedom with international terrorism and launched a **Strike Hard** campaign against 'separatist terrorist forces' resulting in arrests and executions. Other religions, like Falun Gong (a movement that blends Taoism, Buddhism and Qigong exercises) and Christian 'house churches', are banned as cults and a threat to state security. Followers are arrested, detained and sent to Re-education through Labour camps.

Freedom of the Person

An accused person in China does not have the right to a lawyer, to know the evidence against them or to speak in their own defence. People can be sent to prison camp under **Laojiao (Re-Education through Labour)** without a trial, or psychiatric hospitals run by PSB. Those sentenced to **Laogai (Reform through Labour)** face harsh conditions often doing dangerous jobs. China has death penalty for over sixty crimes and executes more people each year than all other countries. China is criticised for harvesting the organs of those it executes.

"Unlawful deprivation or restriction of citizens' freedom of person by detention or other means is prohibited."

Chinese Constitution—Article 37

Equal Rights

Traditionally in China women are considered less important than men. The Politburo has only one female member, **Liu Yandong**, and 60% of unemployed and 70% of the illiterate in China are women. Girls and women have also been kidnapped to sell as forced labour or brides. With the **One Child Policy** many families prefer a boy and male births now outnumber female. Strict enforcement of the One Child Policy has caused riots in some areas and the blind activist, **Chen Guangcheng**, was imprisoned for exposing forced abortions and sterilisations in Shangdong Province in 2005. The Government plans to continue the policy, but has relaxed the rules for second marriages where one partner is childless. In other cases, people pay fines for having more than one child, leading to resentment that the wealthy can easily afford to have another child.

"Women in the People's Republic of China enjoy equal rights with men"

Chinese Constitution—Article 48

Quick Test

1. In what ways is freedom of expression is limited in China?

2. Describe the Chinese Government's policy towards religion and explain its actions in Tibet and Xinjiang.

3. Why has China been criticised for its treatment of prisoners and women?

4. Explain why human rights issues are a problem for China.

Political Structure

Federal System of Government

America is a union of fifty states and has a **federal** system of government. To prevent any single part of the government becoming too powerful, the **US Constitution** sets out the rules for the **separation of the powers** of government into **executive (President), legislative (Congress)** and **judicial (Supreme Court)** branches. It also gives the 50 states the power to look after their own affairs.

STATE AND FEDERAL GOVERNMENT IN THE USA

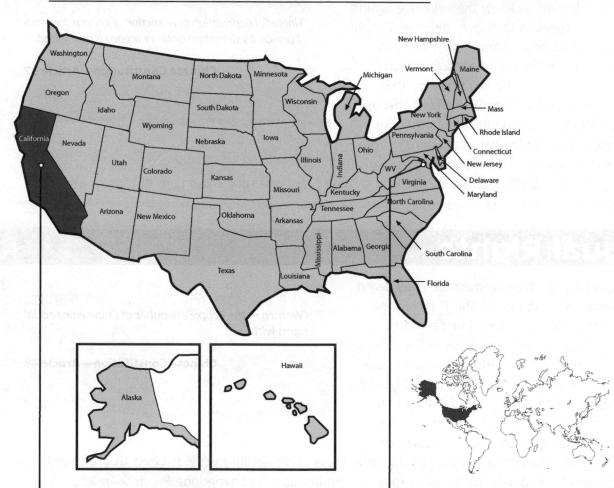

State Government
Example - California

Each state has its own elected government making laws on education, housing, health, etc.

Executive - Governor - maximum of two 4-year terms. The current governor is Arnold Schwarzenegger.
Legislature - The California State Senate (upper house) - 40 members serving four year terms. California State Assembly (lower house) - 80 members serving maximum of three two-year terms (six years).
Judiciary - Supreme Court of California - 7 judges (3 of whom are minorities).

Federal Government
Based in Washington DC

Makes laws for the whole country. Solely responsible for defence and foreign affairs.

Executive - President elected every 4 years (maximum of two 4-year terms).
Legislature - Congress - Senate - 2 Senators from each state - 6 year term with one-third elected every 2 years (no maximum) and House of Representatives - 435 members, elected every 2 years (no maximum) - number from each state depends on size of the population.
Judiciary - Supreme Court of 9 judges appointed for their lifetime by the President and confirmed the Senate - ensures that laws are within the US Constitution.

Electoral College

The system of election for the President of the USA requires a candidate to win at least 270 votes in the **Electoral College**. In most states, the candidate who wins the most votes in a state (the popular vote) gets all the Electoral College votes from that state.

The number of Electoral College votes from each state is the same as their number of Senators and Representatives in Congress. The states with larger populations have more electors – California has 55, while Vermont has only 3. Rather than campaigning nationally, Presidential election campaigns tend to concentrate on winning the popular vote in the states that choose the majority of the electors.

Candidate	Party	Electoral College Votes	Popular Vote	Percentage of Vote
USA Presidential results, 2004 and 2008				
2004 Presidential election result				
George W Bush	Republican	286	59,841,500	51.0%
John Kerry	Democrat	252	56,383,000	48.0%
2008 Presidential election result				
John McCain	Republican	173	58,421,377	45.9%
Barack Obama	Democrat	365	67,066,915	52.7%

Source: *BBC news*

Note that the percentages of votes don't add up to 100%. This is because independent candidates such as Ralph Nader also stand in the elections and win some votes, even when they know they will not win the election.

The 2008 Presidential was clearly a landslide victory. Although Obama achieved a narrow majority of the popular vote he won the majority of the Electoral College votes, and therefore became President.

If no candidate wins a majority of the electoral votes, the House of Representatives will choose the President.

Top Tip
Though this is not examined specifically in the exam, a good understanding of the US political system is important.

Quick Test

1. Describe the three branches of Federal Government.

2. Name some of the representatives Americans have in government?

3. What conclusions can be drawn from the 2004 and 2008 Presidential election results?

4. What are the differences between State and Federal government?

Immigration

There are approximately **305 million** people in the United States of America, with more immigrants arriving each year. The USA's immigrant population, legal and illegal, reached a record 38 million in 2007.

Reasons for Immigration

- The **capitalist ideology and economic system** has made the USA one of the wealthiest nations in the world with a very high standard of living.
- **American Dream** – people believe in the idea that no matter who you are, or where you come from, if you work hard you can make a **success** of your life in the USA.
- **Democracy** – immigrants may want to escape from war and political oppression in their own countries to democratic America which has a written constitution detailing their rights.

Arguments For and Against Immigration

For	Against
USA is a nation of immigrants who came to America to work hard and enjoy the **'American Dream'**, like millions before them.	Immigration places huge **strain on welfare services** in states like California, Texas and Florida where many immigrants settle.
Immigrants contribute to the **economy** because they fill the kind of jobs that most Americans will not take. Their low wages keep prices in the US low and immigrants also pay taxes.	May cause **unemployment** because immigrants are highly concentrated in certain industries, creating competition for a limited number of jobs.
Make USA a **multi-racial**, culturally diverse society.	Increase in **racial prejudice** and violence; more support for groups with racist views, like the Ku Klux Klan.

Responses to Immigration

After 9/11, new legislation in the form of the **Border Security Act** (2001) and the **USA PATRIOT Act** (2001) restricted and controlled the entry of immigrants into the USA. The fenced portion of the **US border** has increased significantly and the number of **Border Patrol agents** has more than doubled in recent years to over 16,500. **Worksite enforcement,** such as the **E-Verify Programme** implemented in states like Arizona, has imposed stricter rules by forcing companies to screen workers to see if they are authorised to work in the country. Many state governments have passed **propositions** that prevent illegal immigrants from receiving welfare and social services. The Department for Homeland Security recently piloted **Operation Scheduled Departure** in five US cities including San Diego and Chicago – it assists illegal immigrants to leave the country. Stronger immigration enforcement, the rejection of amnesty for illegal immigrants by Congress in 2007 and the slowdown in the American economy has reduced illegal immigration from 12.5 million in 2007 to 11.2 million in 2008 – a decline of 11%.

Top Tip
The US Government has introduced many policies to deal with the issue of immigration.

Population Distribution

Ethnic Groups

Blacks / African Americans

The majority of Blacks live in the **South** for historical reasons – **slavery.** Over half of all African Americans are concentrated in the **former slave owning states** of Louisiana, Mississippi, Alabama, Georgia, and South Carolina. Many migrated to the **North** in search of jobs and to escape discrimination but this movement has reversed to some extent, with increasing numbers returning to work in newer industries that have set up in the South.

Hispanics (Latinos)

Over 90% of Mexican Hispanics are concentrated in the **Western** and **Southern** **border-states** of Texas, Arizona, Colorado, New Mexico and California which are the **nearest**

Ethnic groups in USA (2007)

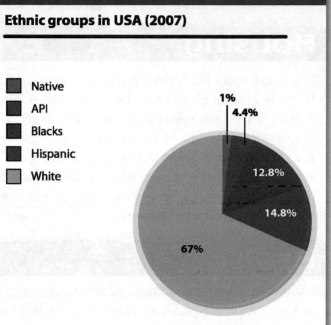

- ■ Native
- ■ API
- ■ Blacks
- ■ Hispanic
- ■ White

1%
4.4%
12.8%
14.8%
67%

Source: *US Census Bureau*

point of entry from Mexico. The majority of **Puerto Ricans**, who do not need a visa for entry to US, live in the Mid-Atlantic states such as **New York** which are closest to Puerto Rico. **Cubans** have settled in **Florida** because it is the closest point of entry and because there is an established community who speak Spanish and have done well economically.

API (Asian and Pacific Islanders)

Over half of APIs are concentrated in the **West** – mostly California. Historical reasons include immigrants being brought to work on the Union Pacific railway in the West Coast. It also remains the closest point of entry from the Pacific. Around a third, including Vietnamese immigrants in Florida, settled in the South because of the similarities in climate and the availability of service sector jobs. Just over half of all APIs live in **wealthier suburbs** because they are in high earning white collar jobs.

Native Americans / Native Indians

Over a third of Native Americans are concentrated on reservations in states such as Arizona, Utah, Colorado, Wyoming and California. Many have migrated to urban areas in pursuit of employment.

Impact of settlement patterns

Ethnic minorities make up **over half** of the population of the large cities. **'White flight'**, where better-off Whites leave the cities to live in **'vanilla' suburbs** and race barriers leave minorities trapped in inner city ghettos, accounts for this. In addition, new immigrants tend to settle in cities because they want to **live** near their **own population groups**.

Quick Test

1. For what reasons do immigrants want to settle in the USA?

2. What are the arguments for and against immigration?

3. Explain why ethnic groups are unevenly distributed across the United States of America.

Social Inequalities and Responses

Housing

Blacks are more likely than Whites to live in poorer housing. The majority of urban Blacks and Hispanics live in **ghettos** in the inner city because they cannot afford better quality housing. The bulk of **urban homeless** also tend to be Black. Minorities are less likely to own their property because they tend to be in low paid jobs – the **credit crunch** may worsen the situation because financial institutions like banks have reduced the amount of credit (loans) for first time buyers. **White flight**, and **growing Black middle class flight**, has reduced tax revenue, so cities do not have money to tackle inner city housing conditions.

Health

The health care costs of most Americans are met by **private health insurance** which they pay for, or their employer provides. Minorities are less likely to have **health insurance** than Whites because they cannot afford it, or are not in jobs which provide it. Therefore, health indicators such as life expectancy, infant mortality, coronary heart disease and cancer, remain higher for certain minorities. Lifestyle factors – smoking, drinking, taking drugs, eating junk food – and poverty have a significant impact on the health of minorities. Tackling socio-economic disadvantage lies at the heart of improving the health status of minorities.

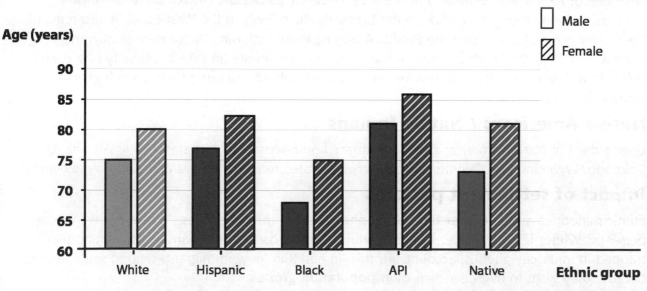

Life Expectancy by Ethnic Origin and Gender (2007)

Source: *US Census Bureau*

Under the Bush administration, the population without health insurance increased to 47 million – an increase in unemployment and the growth of the young Hispanic population account for this. Some states like Massachusetts have made health coverage compulsory and provided subsidies so low income families can buy insurance. Federal responses have included **Health Savings Accounts** which offer tax relief to people who pay for health insurance.

Education

White Americans usually live in areas with good schools, with some being able to afford private education and many going on to higher education. While Black Americans are making progress in education, some are disadvantaged by social and economic inequalities. Ghetto schools tend to have a **'blackboard jungle' image** with high-drop out and low academic success rates. In response, a growing number of states are extending parental choice and providing **tax credits** for working parents who pay for private school tuition for their children. Congress passed (by 1 vote) the first federally-funded **school voucher programme**, known as the **Opportunity Scholarship Programme**, supporting low income households, mainly minorities, with the cost of private schooling. However, only 11% of eligible low income students have applied for the scholarship. Fewer Blacks and Hispanics graduate from college and university so similar measures exist at further education level.

The **College Opportunity and Affordability Act** (2008) doubled the grants available to students and increased funding for colleges serving low income and minority students.

The **No Child Left Behind Act** (2001) which set strict targets for schools, moving students from poorly performing schools to 'good' schools had limited success in improving attainment for minorities. While API progress has been significant, **language barriers** continue to remain a problem for some Hispanic Americans, especially those who have arrived recently or whose parents only speak Spanish at home.

Top Tip

Differences in social inequality exist between and within ethnic groups.

Crime and Law

Black and Hispanic crime statistics are likely to be worse than white crime statistics because crime is concentrated in **inner cities.** Many Black children grow up **'street wise'** against a background of poverty, drugs, prostitution and crime. Blacks and Hispanics feel they face discrimination and prejudice from the police and courts – despite making up only 12% of the population, nearly 50% of prison inmates are Black.

Victims of crime also tend to be minorities – nearly half of all murder victims are Black. This is partly because of gang violence prevalent in inner city ghettos. State and local responses to crime vary across the nation with some opting for harsher measures.

The **Gang Abatement and Prevention Act (2007)** with the **Gang Intervention and Suppression Act (2007)** have made state law crimes into federal offences, carrying more severe penalties.

Quick Test

1. Describe the features of a ghetto.

2. Why do some ethnic groups in the USA do less well in education than others?

3. Explain why there are inequalities in health among ethnic groups in the USA.

4. Describe measures put in place to improve the social progress of minorities in the USA.

Economic Inequalities and Responses

Employment and Unemployment

Blacks and Hispanics have a higher rate of **unemployment** than Whites because they tend to have lower levels of attainment and often face discrimination by employers. Many Hispanics are illegal immigrants and some do not speak fluent English. This makes it difficult to secure a well paid job. However, America is a **less racist** place than it was fifty years ago and many minorities are in top jobs. **Better education,** especially for APIs, has led to improved job prospects and greater earning potential. Many APIs work in **white collar jobs** in 'sunrise' industries, such as electronics.

Income and Poverty

The average income for Whites is higher than for Blacks and Hispanics because minorities are generally found to be in low paid work. Consequently, poverty rates are higher. A large number of Hispanics live in extended families and pool their resources to avoid poverty. While **Temporary Assistance for Needy Families** (TANF) and state support may have helped lift some out of poverty, inequality continues to exist.

Top Tip
The US welfare state encourages its citizens to look after themselves.

Average weekly earnings of full-time workers (2007)

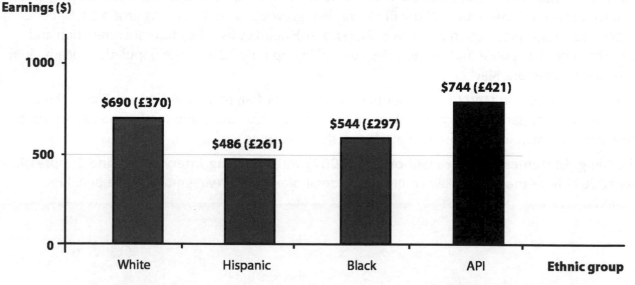

Earnings ($)

- White: $690 (£370)
- Hispanic: $486 (£261)
- Black: $544 (£297)
- API: $744 (£421)

Ethnic group

Source: *US Bureau of Labor Statistics*

Earlier solutions to tackle economic inequalities included **Affirmative Action** programmes – awarding contracts to minority owned businesses, promotion and recruitment policies, and **minority university admission schemes** – to help minorities overcome discrimination. This allowed opportunities, especially for Black Americans, to further their social and economic status by undoing the wrongs of previous discriminatory practices. However, this **preferential** treatment of minorities over suitably qualified Whites was challenged in the Supreme Court and deemed **unconstitutional**. It was opposed on the basis of discrimination because it promotes less qualified individuals.

Why Inequalities Continue

Economic Reasons

'White flight' has meant Whites now pay tax in suburbs outside the cities and as a direct result inner city areas suffer. This has also been a trend among middle class African Americans whose 'Black Flight' has meant few Black role models in inner cities. Recent American Governments have reduced **welfare** which has hit minorities hardest because many rely on the benefit system.

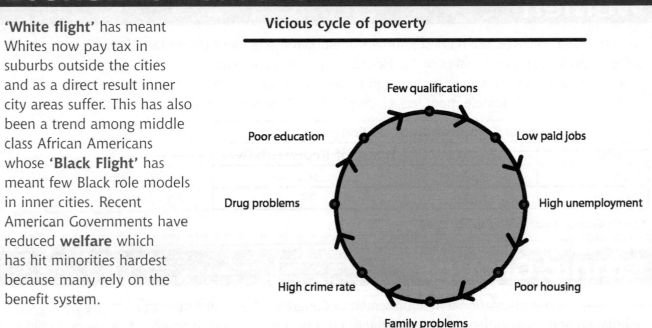

Vicious cycle of poverty

Few qualifications — Low paid jobs — High unemployment — Poor housing — Family problems — High crime rate — Drug problems — Poor education

Social Reasons

Many people from minority groups are stuck in a **'Vicious Cycle Of Poverty'** from which they cannot break free. For young people there are very **few** positive role models, which can lead to a sense of **disenchantment** where people feel they are not valued members of the community. **Discrimination** still exists in jobs, housing and education. This has made it difficult to improve living standards.

Political Reasons

Most minorities feel that the political system has been failed them and this has resulted in **low participation** and under-representation. Political parties cannot completely heal inequality because it will **cost too much**, and this would involve raising taxes which would be unpopular. Also, inequality relates to attitudes. Negative attitudes towards minorities can only be changed through time and education.

Quick Test

1. Why do some members of ethnic groups in the USA find it harder than others to get a job?
2. For what reasons do economic inequalities continue to exist in the USA?
3. What economic progress has been made by minorities in the USA?
4. What are the arguments for and against Affirmative Action?

Representation

Despite being a **multi-cultural society, ethnic minorities** and **women** are **under-represented** at state and national level.

Women

The 2008 elections saw the highest numbers of women elected and Democrat, Nancy Pelosi became the first female Speaker of the House. However, women make up 54% of the US population and if women were represented in proportion to their population size, there would be 54 Senators and 235 female members of the House of Representatives.

Gender Composition of US Congress		
Gender	Senate	House of Representatives
Men	83	361
Women	17	74

Source: *Congressional Demographics, 2008*

Ethnic Groups

Minorities are not proportionately represented in Congress. They make up a third of the US population and if minorities were represented in proportion to their population size, there would be 33 Senators and 143 ethnic minority members of the House of Representatives. There are 91 male Governors and only 8 female Governors – 3 Republicans and 5 Democrats.

Ethnic Composition of US Congress		
Ethnic group	Senate	House of Representatives
White	94	365
Hispanics	3	23
Blacks	1	42
API	2	4
Natives	0	1

Source: *Congressional Demographics, 2008*

Top Tip
Ethnic and gender composition of Congress often does not change even though a third of the Senate stands for election every 2 years.

Age

The average age of Senators in 2008 was 62 years – the youngest Senator is in his forties.

Age Composition of US Congress		
Age	Senate	House of Representatives
30s	–	16
40s	9	79
50s	28	155
60s	37	143
70s >	26	42

Source: *Congressional Demographics, 2008*

Reasons for Under-Representation

Financial barriers – a lack of money remains the most pressing problem for **minorities, women** and **younger candidates**. At state and national level most candidates spend millions of dollars on election campaigns to secure their victory. The income difference between White males and these groups is considerable – this may account for White male dominance in elections. Poverty levels and higher rates of unemployment for Blacks and Hispanics account for the low level of representation at Federal level. Many APIs choose not to stand as candidates, preferring to work in business. Those minorities that do stand often do not gain election because of discrimination on the part of voters. The electoral system and settlement patterns of minorities mean that people are more likely to vote for someone who belongs to the cultural or ethnic group with which they identify.

Responses to Under-Representation

Minority representation increased following the introduction of **majority-minority districts** in the 1990s. This changed the distict boundaries, creating areas with large Black or Hispanic population groups and increasing the likelihood of minority candidates being elected.

Black Representatives in the House are Democrats - collectively known as the **Black Caucus** (group) – have a degree of infuence in Congress because they have **over** 20% of the votes needed for a bill to pass as legislation.

Since his election in 2000, and re-election in 2004, George Bush has appointed Cabinet members who more accurately reflect the broad racial diversity of the US population. He appointed **Condoleezza Rice**, an African American female, as Secretary of State in his Cabinet. Other prominent and influential politicians have included Colin Powell. These positive role models may inspire others to stand as candidates.

The **2008 Presidential Election** campaign had a female, a minority and a 72-year old candidate competing in the primaries. This highlights the emerging, more representative nature of American politics. The election of the first minority President, Barack Obama, may inspire other minorities to put themselves forward as candidates.

In 2008, Barack Obama was elected the first Black President of the USA

Quick Test

1. Describe the ways in which women in the USA are under-represented in the political system.
2. Explain why ethnic minorities in the USA continue to face inequality of representation in the political system.
3. What measures have been put in place to improve ethnic minority representation?
4. How does the 2008 Presidential Election differ from previous elections?

Participation

Voter Registration

In the USA the responsibility for **voter registration** lies with individuals. The **National Voter Registration Act** – otherwise known as the '**Motor Voter Act**' – obliged states to offer registration at government offices when applying for, or renewing, a driving licence. The reduced **barriers to registration** clearly make it easier to participate in elections, but do not in themselves increase the motivation to vote. While the process is now more convenient, different states have different rules and proceduresMany minorities are **intimidated** by the process, especially where offices are far from their homes, or where they are required to produce their identity card, social security number or driving licence.

	Voting Turnout by Ethnic Group				
	2004 Presidential Election		2008 Presidential Election		
	Total Ballots Cast: 122,295,345		Total Ballots Cast: 126,276,331		
Ethnic Group	**Exit Poll**	**Estimated Total Ballots**	**Exit Poll**	**Estimated Total Ballots**	
White	77%	94,167,000	74%	93,444,000	
African American	11%	13,452,000	13%	16,416,000	
Hispanic	8%	9,784,000	9%	11,365,000	
API	2%	2,446,000	2%	2,526,000	
Other	2%	2,446,000	3%	3,788,000	

Source: Fereral Election Commission, 2008

The **Unity 04 Campaign** did a great deal to increase voter registration among African Americans. Alongside celebrities, the Unity 04 Campaign organised voter registration at churches, salons and college campuses. **Your Voice is Your Vote** stressed the importance of participating in elections to Hispanic voters by contacting them by post, phone and email. Measures such as **10-4 Campaign** and **Campaign for Communities** increased the Hispanic vote.

Voting

Elections are important because they allow American citizens to **participate** in choosing their local and national political representatives. Opportunities to vote include:

- **Federal** level – the electorate can vote for the **President** every 4 years. They can also vote for **Senators** every 6 years.
- **State** level – the electorate can vote for a **Governor** - head of State Government.
- **Local** level – the electorate can vote for the **Mayor**.

Voter turnout has remained low, particularly for women, minorities and young people. Difficulties of registration are only part of the reason. Many are **disillusioned** with the political process and politicians. Reports of discrimination through corruption of the electoral process further strengthened this claim. However, the **Help America Vote Act (2002)** aimed to boost citizens' confidence in the electoral process by updating voting procedures. Minorities continue to face social and economic inequality despite having voted for politicians who promised to address inequalities. In addition, there is a correlation (link) between educational attainment and voting; poorly educated individuals who drop out of school are less likely to vote. New immigrants are less inclined to vote because of their status (they might be illegal) or because English is their second language. However, election campaigns now report in Spanish, and both the Democrats and Republicans are targeting the **minority vote** by producing their electoral publications in Spanish.

Standing as a Candidate

Americans can stand as candidates for political posts, and more minorities and women are standing as candidates at local and state level because they feel that they have a greater chance of success. The majority of candidates tend to belong to the two main political parties who are able to fund election campaigns and finance air time. In addition, there are certain requirements for wanting to hold public office e.g. be at least 25 and reside in the state for 7 years for wanting to stand as a US Senator.

Political Parties

The **Republican Party** and the **Democratic Party** dominate politics. Many people campaign for these parties by handing out leaflets and posters giving the candidate's name, party and main policies. They organise **fund raising events** and are increasingly using the internet to rally voters.

The 2008 Presidential Election attracted many first time campaigners – Barack Obama and Hillary Clinton rallied their supporters during the primaries. There are now around **80 million** registered Democrat supporters and **60 million** registered Republican supporters.

Democratic Party symbol

Republican Party symbol

Interest Groups

Americans can join, and campaign, for an **interest group** such as the **National Rifle Association (NRA)** which campaigns for the right to carry a gun. Many people have campaigned by signing petitions, taking part in demonstrations and contacting the media.

Interest groups can be very influential in US politics with many having close links to members of the House and the Senate. They hire **professional lobbyists** who influence decision making in Congress by contacting influential politicians. They donate millions of dollars to election campaigns at state and federal level to elect candidates who support their views.

Allegations of corruption and lack of accountability (people not taking responsibility for their decisions) led Congress to pass the **Honest Leadership and Open Government Act** in 2007.

Quick Test

1. What type of representatives can Americans vote for?
2. What measures have been introduced to encourage voter registration?
3. How can individuals participate in interest groups?
4. Why do many Americans not vote in elections?

Integration

The European Union (EU), originally called the European Economic Community (EEC), was set up by six Western European countries who signed the Treaty of Rome in 1957. Among the main reasons for this was the belief that co-operation between states would reduce the likelihood of another war in Europe and help rebuild war damaged economies. Originally the UK decided not to join this group and only became part of the EU in 1973. Membership of the EU now stands at 27 member countries.

European Union Member States

The European Union created a **single market**. This single market has three key features:

1. **A free trade area** allows free movement of goods and services. This has involved removing all restrictions on imports such as tariffs and quotas between member states and agreeing a common set of product, health and safety standards.

2. **A customs union** has been established. This means that a **common external tariff** has been agreed, i.e. all members charge the same tariffs on goods imported from countries outside the EU.

3. **A single factor market** allows free movement of resources such as capital and labour between member countries. Citizens of EU member states can live and work in any other EU country.

Complete **harmonisation** has not yet been achieved in the 'single market'. Differences remain in VAT, excise duties, taxes on company profits, income tax and the move towards **a single currency** and **full monetary union**.

Single Market

The development of the EU can be seen as a series of stages of economic and political integration between member nations and also an expansion of the size of the single market. The single market brings benefits to both consumers and producers. The lack of import controls like tariffs reduces prices of goods and services which boosts consumers' real living standards. The enormous size of the single market with a population of nearly 500 million people might allow businesses to expand their scale of production and benefit from **economies of scale**. Producing a large volume of output leads to lower costs and price for consumers.

The single market is a powerful and important free trade area in the world. The European Union accounts for a large percentage of world trade in goods and services.

Arguments For and Against Integration

For	Against
The EU safeguards peace as European nations are now locked into reliance with each another. The EU has helped to bring political stability and therefore it is highly unlikely that member states would enter into armed conflict with one another.	The EU is costly for well-off nations like the UK because the cost of being a member is greater than the benefits they get. Some estimates suggest that the annual net cost to the UK of EU membership is around £40 billion.
EU membership gives states increased influence on the global stage. While other nations would find it easy to ignore Britain, or any European nation acting on its own, the combined influence of all twenty-seven member states acting together is harder to dismiss.	The EU is becoming too powerful. It is able to make decisions that can override UK laws. This process has been accelerated in recent years since the emergence of international terrorism.
The EU has made member states better off by reducing barriers to trade like tariffs. Increased trade creates employment and stimulates the economy.	The EU is undemocratic and unaccountable to people. Most EU decisions are made by the EU Commission which is led by unelected Commissioners.

Share of World Trade

The charts show the levels of world trade in goods and services (imports and exports) between the EU member states and other parts of the world.

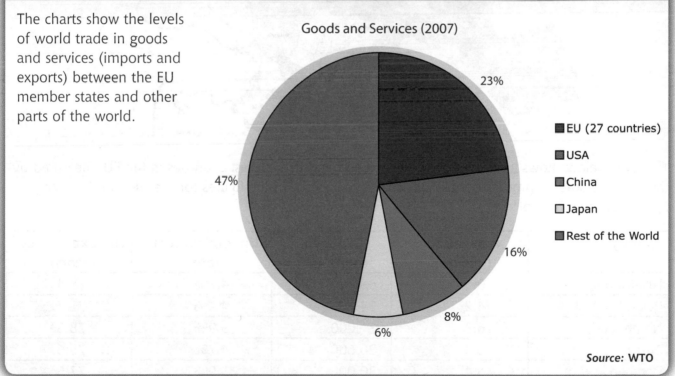

Goods and Services (2007)

23%

47%

16%

8%

6%

- EU (27 countries)
- USA
- China
- Japan
- Rest of the World

Source: WTO

Quick Test

1. Why was the European Union created?
2. Describe some advantages for countries that are members of the European Union.
3. What conclusions can be drawn about the EU's role in world trade?
4. Why has complete harmonisation not taken place?

Comparisons Between EU States

The European Union is made up of 27 member states with different economic, social, political and cultural traditions.

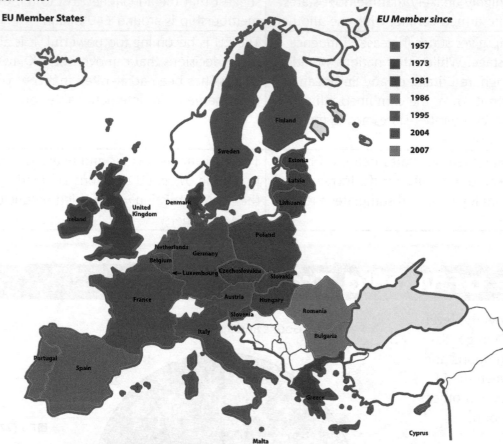

EU Member States

EU Member since
- 1957
- 1973
- 1981
- 1986
- 1995
- 2004
- 2007

The table below shows indicators for the five richest and five poorest countries in the EU, measured by their Gross Domestic product per person. The table also shows the figures for the UK and the average figures for the whole of the EU.

Country	Population (million)	GDP per capita (€)	Unemployment rate	Life expectancy (years)
Luxembourg	0.5	66,100	4.7%	78.4
Ireland	4.2	34,100	4.4%	77.7
Netherlands	16.3	31,000	3.9%	78.8
Austria	8.3	30,600	4.7%	78.6
Denmark	5.4	30,000	3.9%	77.5
United Kingdom	**60**	**28,200**	**5.3%**	**77.6**
Lithuania	3.4	13,700	5.6%	70.7
Latvia	2.3	13,300	6.8%	70.4
Poland	38.2	12,600	13.8%	74.3
Romania	21.6	8,900	7.3%	72.1
Bulgaria	7.7	8,800	9.0%	72.3
EU	493.1	23,700	7.9%	76.3

Edinburgh and Warsaw

Top Tip
Your teacher may have provided different examples of communities in the EU to compare and contrast. Don't worry if Edinburgh and Warsaw are not your own centre's examples.

Edinburgh

Population – 468,070 (2007)

Population Groups:
Scottish 77%
English 12%
Polish 2%
Aslan 3%
Others 6%

GDP per capita (2008) £28,432

Unemployment (2008) 2.2%

Employment – education, health, finance, business services, retailing, tourism, brewing, publishing.

Education – 4 Universities.

Housing – the average price of a house in Edinburgh is just over £220,000 making it the most expensive city in Scotland. The majority of people own their homes; with the remainder living in council or privately rented accommodation. There is a large student population therefore student flats are common.

Family Life – nuclear family remains the most common family structure, high student population and many cohabiting couples.

Leisure – theatres, museums, art galleries, parks and gardens, historic monuments.

International Festivals – Edinburgh Festival, Film Festival, Book Festival, Tattoo, Hogmanay, museums, theatre, clubs, pubs, zoo, shopping, football, rugby.

Warsaw

Population – 1,704,717 [2008]

GDP per capita (2008) £21,500

Unemployment (2008) 5.1%

Employment – steel, car manufacture, electronics, food processing, retail, tourism.

Average monthly salary £723

Education – All Polish children attend school between the ages of 6 and 18. There are five stages of schooling – pre-schools, elementary schools, lower secondary schools, upper secondary schools and higher education. Many children attend private schools in Warsaw.

4 universities

255,000 university students

500,000 school pupils

29.2% of the population

20% of population have a university degree.

Housing – the average price of a house in Warsaw varies depending on its size; £2,700 per square metre. Luxury houses have been constructed as the result of an emerging affluent class.

Family Life – the nuclear family is getting smaller in Warsaw, but the extended family is still central in Polish life.

Leisure – football, theatres, museums, art galleries, film production.

Enlargement

The European Union expanded to twenty five nations in May 2004 with the **accession of ten countries.** Bulgaria and Romania joined the EU in January 2007 to take the total to twenty seven and Croatia, Macedonia and Turkey are all classified as **candidate countries** seeking membership. The result has been a **widening** of the Single European market. In order to qualify for membership, candidate countries must meet the **Copenhagen criteria**, which set standards for democracy, human rights, a market economic system, and the integration of European law into judicial system.

Advantages of Enlargement to Current Members

Employment – new immigrants are taking jobs which British people do not want or cannot fill. For example, shortages in skilled trades, dentists and health care workers are being filled by many Polish immigrants. They are helping to relieve supply bottlenecks in the UK economy and helping to reduce inflationary pressure in areas of full employment.

Demography – the population of the UK is declining and therefore the country needs a net influx of workers to contribute to the economy to tackle growing issues like the ageing population. The revenue generated in income tax and indirect taxes, like VAT, help to fund the welfare state.

Single market – free trade of goods and services within the EU through the removal of trade barriers, like tariffs and quotas, has given UK consumers greater choice. In addition, UK businesses have increased exports to new EU member states.

Advantages of Enlargement to New Members

Single market – access to the single market and overseas capital is likely to promote employment and living standards. For example, real GDP growth in Latvia is 8.5% compared to UK's 3%. Businesses may set up factories in new member states. There has been an increase in foreign direct investment into accession countries because they have lower tax rates e.g. Lithuania has a 15% tax rate on company profits compared to 30% in the UK.

Freedom of movement – for individuals to live, work and study within any EU member state has raised the standard of living for many individuals from poorer nations.

Regional Development – new members have access to assistance from the Regional Development Fund. This is of great benefit in helping to develop economies of new members and bringing them up to the standard of the more established members.

Common Agricultural Policy – some of the states that wish to join depend considerably on agriculture. They would benefit from the Common Agricultural Policy (CAP), which provides grants and subsidies to improve equipment and production methods on farms. New markets would open up for goods produced in applicant countries and people could look for work in any country in the EU.

Disadvantages of Enlargement for Current Members

Unemployment – new migrants from countries like Poland and Hungary are taking jobs in more established member states, such as Britain. In addition, businesses in some EU countries could face competition from the new members. Wage costs are lower in most of the new countries than in the rest of the EU, so their prices may be cheaper. In addition, investment is moving to new members because their tax rates remain favourable to businesses.

Welfare state – many people argue that new immigrants drain the welfare state by claiming benefits and using services such as the NHS. Evidence shows that the percentage of Eastern Europeans claiming UK benefits like income support and Job Seekers Allowance remains low.

EU budget – The costs of CAP, Regional Aid, and Structural Funds will increase over the years as a result of enlargement. Regional development for new members means fewer funds for older members. Most of the new members have a low level of GDP per capita compared to the existing members. Under the recent EU budget deal, the UK's **net contribution** to the EU will increase by 63%, from £3.5bn a year to £6bn a year during 2006–2013.

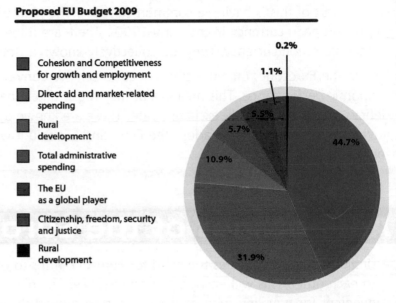

Proposed EU Budget 2009

- Cohesion and Competitiveness for growth and employment
- Direct aid and market-related spending
- Rural development
- Total administrative spending
- The EU as a global player
- Citizenship, freedom, security and justice
- Rural development

0.2%
1.1%
5.5%
5.7%
10.9%
44.7%
31.9%

Source: **European Commission**

Disadvantages of Enlargement for New Members

Competition – The threat of inexpensive competition from another member state may cause the closure of businesses and higher unemployment. There are economic concerns about the ability of poorer Eastern European countries to compete with more economically advanced member states.

Migration – The impact on people migrating to member states in the hope of securing a better lifestyle for their families may be difficult. There could be an increase racial tension. For example, there has been an increase in the number of **faceless racist incidents** in the UK involving white Europeans attacking other White Europeans. In addition, countries like Poland have faced labour shortages because many talented and skilled workers have left for the UK.

Quick Test

1. What recent developments has the EU experienced with regard to membership?
2. Describe the advantages for existing member states of an increased single market.
3. Describe the impact of enlargement on the movement of resources.
4. What conclusions can be drawn about the proposed budget for 2009?

Single European Currency

Background

To achieve a complete single market, the EU is moving towards Economic and Monetary Union (EMU). Part of this is having a common currency. The Maastricht Treaty laid down proposals for a single European currency in the early 1990s. There are fifteen EU states who have adopted the Euro as their common currency. They are collectively known as the **Eurozone**.

To join the Eurozone, member states need to achieve **convergence** of their economic policies and economic performance. This means that they must match their inflation rates, interest rates, budget deficits, and have a stable exchange rate. These are known as the **convergence criteria**. The UK government decided not to adopt the Euro, and has said it will only do so if the British people vote for the Euro in a referendum.

Advantages of the Euro

A single currency eliminates the need for Eurozone firms to convert currencies when they trade with each other. This will encourage trade between member countries. In addition, it is also more convenient for travellers who no longer need to convert their currency.

A single currency eliminates the problem of fluctuating exchange rates between Eurozone currencies and this will reduce uncertainty for firms. This creates an economic climate whereby trade flourishes. Nearly 60% of UK trade in goods and services is conducted with other members of the European Union.

There will be greater price transparency which may lead to **cheaper trade**. Consumers will be able to make direct comparisons of prices for the same products in different countries and put pressure on manufacturers who charge different prices for the same product in different markets, e.g. cars.

Many supporters of the EU, known as **Europhiles**, argue that the Euro is a major step towards an **integrated European Union**. The loss of national sovereignty that many politicians feared has not been a major feature of concern for national citizens.

Disadvantages of the Euro

A single currency removes the advantage of floating exchange rates. If the UK has a trade deficit with the Euro-zone then with a flexible exchange rate the £ would fall against the Euro. The weaker pound would make British goods cheaper for foreign consumers and would make Eurozone goods dearer for British consumers. This would help to reduce the trade deficit.

A common currency requires a **common interest rate**. Governments lose the ability to control their monetary policy – there is a **'one size fits all monetary policy'**. This can create difficulty in an economy which is out of step with others, e.g. the European Central Bank, based in Germany, may lower the rate of interest if most of the EU countries are in recession. If, however, one or more country is in a boom period with rising inflationary pressures then a cut in the rate of interest will make their inflation problem worse.

The European Central Bank

The **European Central Bank (ECB)** is the central bank of the Eurozone. The ECB is responsible for setting interest rates through the Eurozone countries. Its main aim is to maintain stable prices by keeping inflation under control. An independent ECB, free from national political control, is more likely to be a 'safer pair of hands' than national governments, which sometimes use monetary policy for political purposes. During election years, governments have sometimes reduced interest rates to stimulate spending, thereby creating a feel-good factor among consumers. This increases the likelihood of being re-elected.

The European Central Bank headquarters in Frankfurt, Germany

Britain and the Euro

Opinion is divided in Britain over the benefits of joining the Euro. The Government has stated that Britain would have to meet five economic tests before setting a referendum on the issue. The Government is keen to retain a **floating currency** and an **independent monetary policy**. It believes that the Bank of England has done a good job in setting interest rates and controlling inflation.

Quick Test

1. What is the Eurozone?
2. Describe the advantages for travellers of having the Euro.
3. Explain the disadvantages of adopting the Euro.
4. What is the UK's stance on the Euro?

EU Policies

Common Agricultural Policy

The Common Agricultural Policy (CAP) is a central EU policy relating to all farmers in the EU. It exists to provide a reasonable level of income for farmers in order that they produce steady supplies of all main food products. Amongst other elements of the CAP, farmers are paid subsidies to compete against farmers from developing countries in international markets. Modern technology and farming methods are also promoted to enable productivity in agriculture. Consumers in all member states benefit from more choice and stable prices when farmers receive a stable income.

Total CAP spending by country in 2006 (50 bn €)

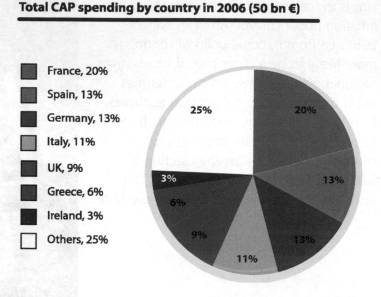

- France, 20%
- Spain, 13%
- Germany, 13%
- Italy, 11%
- UK, 9%
- Greece, 6%
- Ireland, 3%
- Others, 25%

Source: **European Commission**

Despite these benefits, people have criticised CAP for leading to overproduction of some foodstuffs. It suits countries of the EU that have large agricultural sectors, such as France, at the expense of countries that do not, such as the UK. Many people in the UK feel that French farmers are given too much assistance from CAP. The proportion of EU spending on CAP is already high and enlargement of the EU will worsen the situation. Some people argue that money could be better spent to benefit more people. For them, EU spending priorities need to be fundamentally altered to take into account the ever-changing circumstances in which the EU finds itself.

Reform of the CAP

Changes to CAP were essential because of escalating costs for providing agricultural support. In addition, political clashes between nations and mounting pressure from the media were not conducive to creating an integrated EU. During rounds of the World Trade Organisation, the EU was pressurised into reducing import tariffs on agricultural products and cutting export subsidies for nations that retaliated.

The **enlargement of the EU** has accelerated demands for an overhaul of the CAP system. The EU published proposals on CAP in May 2008. The proposals included ways in which the CAP could be modified and simplified so that farmers can respond quickly to the market. For example, the requirement for arable farmers to leave 10% of their land fallow (set-aside) would be abolished so all land can be used to produce food. The amount of direct payments to farmers that are transferred to wider rural development programmes would be increased, particularly for larger farmers.

Common Fisheries Policy

The Common Fisheries Policy was set up to monitor fish stocks, protect the living standards of those employed in the fishing market, and protect consumer interests. The problem for the fishing industry has been a **free rider** problem. No member state owns the seas, so no member can set limits on the amount of fish that can be taken out. This has led to overfishing and depletion of stocks.

In order to maintain stocks, the EU Commission has set maximum fishing catches, known as **quotas**, to allow fish stocks to grow. Restrictions are placed on the number of days and time of year that boats can fish and controls are placed on the size of nets. This will have an effect on the fishing industry in all member states but these effects will not be shared equally because the percentage of the workforce employed in fishing varies.

Although Britain's fishing fleet has been in serious decline for many years, there are still pockets of Scotland which rely heavily on fishing. The Common Fisheries Policy has hit these areas hard. Critics also claim that EU quotas are not fair and some fish have not been included in the ban. French and Spanish fishermen will be allowed to fish for monkfish, sole and prawns off their coastlines. This means that they will continue to make a good living. The free rider problem continues to exist because of enforcement and policing issues of fishing fleets. The SNP Government wants the CFP scrapped.

Regional Policy

One of the key aims of the European Union when it was set up was to improve living standards throughout all the countries of the Union. Some member countries or regions within countries are not as well off as others. Strong regional disparities remain in virtually every EU nation.

Poorer areas have been targeted for special help in the form of regional aid. The **Structural Fund** has four types of funds dealing with training, agriculture, the environment and infrastructure (roads, transport and communications).

In order to qualify for aid, member states must meet the **Objective Status criteria**. Studies are carried out in EU countries to establish income levels and poor areas within countries are targeted for special help. Factors taken into account include unemployment, declining industries and rates of poverty.

The European Union does not give direct financial help to businesses. Instead, it will co-fund projects along with local authorities and regional governments to improve the conditions in an area; making it more attractive for a business to set up there. The theory is that if a business can be attracted into a declining area, it will create jobs, raise income levels and contribute to a higher standard of living throughout the area.

The differences in prosperity within the EU continue to grow as the result of enlargement. In addition, many argue that diverting resources to newer member states may be politically unpopular.

Quick Test

1. Explain why many people want the CAP reformed.
2. Describe the ways in which the EU can help poorer regions of member states.
3. Explain, in detail, the ways in which the Common Fisheries Policy has an effect on EU member states.
4. What conclusions can be drawn about total CAP spending?

Military Co-operation

North Atlantic Treaty Organisation

NATO was set up at the start of the **Cold War** when Europe divided into **communist** and **capitalist** countries. The former Soviet Union set up the **Warsaw Pact** with the communist countries of Eastern Europe and Western Europe set up NATO to stop the spread of communism. It was based on **collective defence** – if one NATO member was attacked **all** other NATO members would come to its aid.

Until the 1990s, the two military alliances faced each other and built up their weapons in a dangerous **Arms Race**. Since then communism has collapsed in Eastern Europe, the Warsaw Pact has disbanded and some of its former members have joined NATO. Many members of NATO are delighted that new members have joined.

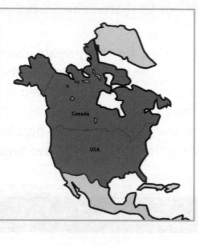

NATO countries in North America and Europe

NATO now has 26 member states with Secretary General Jaap de Hoop Scheffer at its head.

NATO has an open door policy on enlargement. Any European country in a position to contribute to security in the Euro-Atlantic area can become a member of the Alliance, when invited to do so by the existing member countries. Countries aspiring for NATO membership are also expected to meet certain political, economic and military goals.

The last wave of enlargement was in March 2004 when seven nations joined the Alliance (Bulgaria, Estonia, Latvia, Lithuania, Romania, Slovakia and Slovenia), bringing the total membership of the Alliance to 26. NATO and the European Union now have 21 member countries in common.

Increased Membership

For	Against
Will help make the alliance stronger by increasing the number of troops and weapons.	New members with large scale forces often depend on outdated equipment rather than modern technology.
It will help NATO preserve democracy and peace by having a greater number of nations.	It could prove difficult coordinating any action involving so many members and communicating in a number of different languages.
It will be able to act against international terrorism.	There might be problems deciding on an integrated command structure.

EU Military Involvement

Since the collapse of Communism in the late 1980s, the EU has tried to expand its role in defence through the **European Security and Defence Policy** (ESDP) which is part of the Common Foreign and Security Policy (CFSP). The EU's weakness during the 1990s Balkan conflicts, where NATO and the USA led operations, demonstrated the need for EU member states to work together on defence.

The **Berlin Plus Arrangements**, adopted in 2003, strengthened EU-NATO co-operation. The arrangements allow the EU access to NATO's collective assets and capabilities like weapons for EU-led operations. In effect, they allow the alliance to support EU-led operations in which NATO as a whole is not actively engaged. For example, in Kosovo, the EU operation has access to NATO's equipment and command structures. Equally, the EU and NATO have worked together in countries like Afghanistan.

However, there are operations where the EU has acted alone. For example, there are EU armed forces deployed to help keep the peace in the Democratic Republic of the Congo, a former Belgian colony. The presence of European troops in Congo was originally intended to help the country continue its slow steps toward recovery and reconciliation. This has steadily changed to providing Westerners a safe getaway when things fall apart. Added to this are problems with troop numbers. Smaller EU nations such as Belgium, Spain, Poland, Sweden, and Portugal have only made a firm commitment for a few dozen troops each.

European Security and Defence Policy

For	Against
All member states face similar security threats so they should work together to protect each other.	ESDP diverts resources away from existing organisations such as NATO.
The USA can no longer be asked to carry the majority of the burden of defence through NATO – the EU needs to pull its own weight.	The EU's Rapid Reaction Force duplicates NATO's Response Force.
ESDP allows greater freedom for the EU because they are able to pursue their own defence agenda.	The EU continues to turn to its ally to contribute military forces to problems which involve our own security.

Quick Test

1. Why do EU member states continue to cooperate on military matters?
2. Why is NATO important for the protection of EU member states?
3. Explain the main arguments for and against increased membership of NATO.
4. Describe recent EU military involvement.

Regional Differences

Brazil is on the east coast of the continent of South America. It is the fifth largest country in the world, in area and in population, and has one of the largest economies in the world. It has been affected by **economic issues** such as trade, aid and foreign debt. However, **social** and **economic inequality** between groups of people and the **abuse of human rights** continue to exist despite federal, state and local responses.

Brazil is divided into five main regions and one of the most commonly asked questions in exams is about the differences between regions. Below is a summary of information on two regions – the North and the South East.

North and South East Brazil

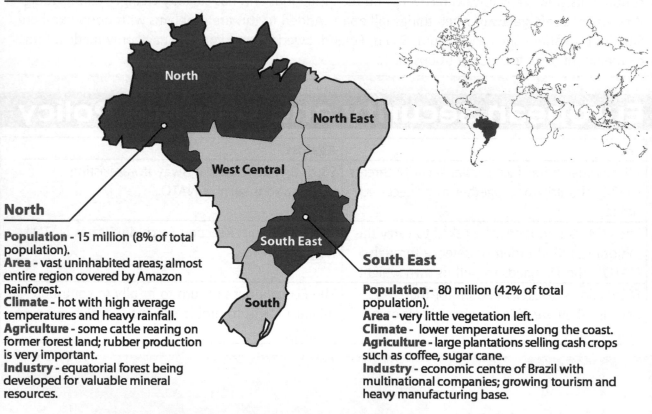

North

Population - 15 million (8% of total population).
Area - vast uninhabited areas; almost entire region covered by Amazon Rainforest.
Climate - hot with high average temperatures and heavy rainfall.
Agriculture - some cattle rearing on former forest land; rubber production is very important.
Industry - equatorial forest being developed for valuable mineral resources.

South East

Population - 80 million (42% of total population).
Area - very little vegetation left.
Climate - lower temperatures along the coast.
Agriculture - large plantations selling cash crops such as coffee, sugar cane.
Industry - economic centre of Brazil with multinational companies; growing tourism and heavy manufacturing base.

Cultural Features

Ethnic Groups

Brazilians consider themselves as **one people with a single culture**. The original inhabitants of Brazil, **Native Indians**, are the smallest population group followed by **Asians**. The majority of Brazilians are **White** – this is as a result of its **colonial past**, when Portugal ruled Brazil. **Blacks** were originally brought as slaves to work on sugar and coffee plantations. This has led to a growing number of people of **mixed race**, either light skinned **mestico** or dark skinned **mulatto**.

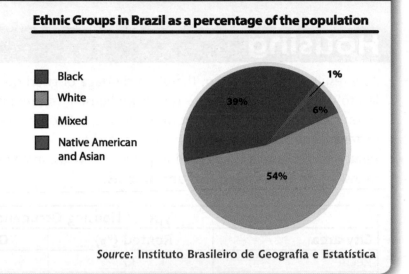

Ethnic Groups in Brazil as a percentage of the population

- Black
- White
- Mixed
- Native American and Asian

39%   1%   6%   54%

Source: **Instituto Brasileiro de Geografia e Estatística**

Religion

The Brazilian constitution guarantees the **freedom of religion**. Around 73% of the population would call themselves **Roman Catholic** – although this number is falling. There are also a **variety of beliefs** held by Native Indians.

Sport and Leisure

Football is the national sport and Brazil will host the 2014 World Cup. Watching rival teams Flamengo and Fluminense battle it out at the Maracana Stadium in Rio de Janeiro is a popular pastime. Other sports such as **volleyball** are popular on the beaches of Brazil's coast. The greatest annual event in Brazil is **Carnival**, which takes place each February.

Food and Drink

Meals are very much social occasions and part of the culture in Brazil. Different regions tend to have their own favourite dishes – **Moqueca** (fish stew) is popular in the North East region. Coffee is the most popular beverage, followed by a variety of **tropical fruit juices.** A popular drink is rum made from sugar cane mixed with lime and sugar called **Caipirinha**.

Quick Test

1. What are the main differences between the North and the South East?
2. Name the main ethnic groups in Brazil.
3. Name one popular food and drink in Brazil.
4. Explain why differences exist between the North and South East.

Social Inequalities and Responses

Housing

As a result of **urbanisation**, there is a shortage of good quality housing in Brazil's cities. This has led to the growth of **favelas** – run down housing communities. Favelas are often built on steep hills, or on marshes, so are at risk from mudslides or flooding. Lack of sewerage systems and running water means that **diseases** such as TB and cholera spread easily. Moreover, growing levels of **crime** related to gangs and drugs is widespread in favelas. In contrast, many wealthier Brazilians live in mansions or **luxury high rise apartments.**

Type of Housing Occupancy (2007)			
City area	Rented (%)	Owned (%)	Favelas (%)
Recife	17	65	18
Salvador	10	74	16
Rio de Janeiro	21	48	31
São Paolo	22	49	29

Source: **Ministries of Cities (Adapted)**

Spending on housing and sanitation by the **Ministry of Cities** has alleviated many housing problems by improving access to the favelas, improving sewerage systems, and providing clean water and electricity. Street numbers have also been assigned to housing units so residents can be regarded as proper citizens. Housing shortages have been reduced by building low cost homes – financed by a loan from the **World Bank**. In addition, the **Residential Lease Programme** allows many disadvantaged families to buy their home. Legalising property rights and **extending title deeds** to families living in favelas has been hugely successful. However, people in favelas find it difficult to improve their living standards because of the constant influx of new inhabitants from rural areas, making it difficult for the government to help existing residents.

Education

The Brazilian Government has made education an important part of their **constitution** and guarantees the right of all Brazilians to eight years of education. Despite this guarantee, 12% of Brazilians aged over 15 years are unable to read and write – one of the highest illiteracy rates in Latin America.

Regional differences exist in enrolment, attendance and literacy, with the South East performing well on all three counts. Differences between urban and rural schools are growing – cities have more resources and teachers who earn higher salaries. However, the government has tried to improve this by increasing spending on education and attempting to distribute resources more **equitably** (fairly).

Racial differences in education also exist. Black and mixed race young adults have illiteracy rates double that of Whites and Asians. This is because the majority of white middle class children attend private schools, with most going on to college and university. Children of poor working class families, the majority of whom are Black and mixed race, rarely finish school and often end up in low paid work.

The **Ministry of Education** has tried to address the problems in education by giving financial support in the form of an educational maintenance allowance called the **Bolsa Escola**. This measure has raised enrolment and attendance. To wipe out illiteracy the government set up '**The Eradication of the Illiteracy Programme**' but funding was slashed and the goal became one of gradual literacy.

Health

Health remains an important priority for the government because of the inequalities that exist between regions and ethnic groups. Blacks have higher rates of illness and mortality than Whites. The South East has favourable health indicators similar to More Economically Developed Countries (MEDCs). The financing of health care has not been sufficient to cover government aims of providing universal and fair treatment. **Hunger** remains a deep rooted problem across Brazil. HIV/AIDS is a significant problem despite successful health programmes.

Fome Zero (Zero Hunger) introduced in 2003 allocates roughly a $15 (£8) allowance per month to each undernourished family. However funding cuts have been made due to the government's debt burden. State authorities are **training** more doctors and nurses but there are differences between regions. The **Community Pharmacy Programme** provides low income families with a wide range of medicines, and the government provides free antiretroviral drugs for the treatment of HIV/AIDS.

Top Tip

Economic pressures from global institutions like the World Bank restricts what Brazilian Government can spend.

Crime

Firearms are the biggest cause of death among Brazil's youth – one person is killed every 15 minutes by a gun. Those living in favelas are likely to be targets of violence and gun crimes, often by **corrupt police officers**. The justice system is widely regarded as ineffective – a slow legal system struggles to cope with the large number of prisoners. Overcrowded, damp and unsanitary conditions, combined with a poor diet and general ill health, has led to an outbreak of TB in Brazilian prisons.

The **Disarmament Act 2003** imposed tougher measures against violence, including tighter gun control. The **Workers Party** (PT) passed a law raising the minimum age for buying a gun from 21 to 25 and punishing those who carry a gun illegally with a **prison sentence**. However, a proposal to ban the sale of firearms was defeated in a referendum. **Community policing schemes** were introduced in Brazil to strengthen community relations between the police and local residents.

Quick Test

1. Describe some of the features of favelas.
2. Describe the inequalities that exist in education in Brazil?
3. For what reasons is crime a serious problem in Brazil?
4. Describe the progress made by poor Brazilians.

Economic Issues

Wealth

Brazil has the largest economy in Latin America and the tenth largest in the world. Consistent economic growth has created wealth in Brazil.

However, Brazil unequally distributes income and wealth. This inequality stems from **land ownership**. Government policies have not addressed these inequalities because global institutions have set restrictions on spending. Despite this, **Bolsa Familia** – a federal scheme that gives cash payments to the poorest – has resulted in the emergence of a new lower middle class in Brazil.

Employment

Agriculture is the largest sector in terms of employment and Brazil is the world's largest exporter of agricultural products – mainly coffee, sugar, soya-beans, orange, beef and cocoa. However, Brazil has faced problems with **foreign trade.** For example, when the prices of agricultural products fall on the international market jobs are lost and people fall into poverty.

Industry is important to Brazil, especially machinery, electrical goods, construction materials, rubber, chemicals and vehicle production. The country also possesses large **mineral reserves**, including iron ore – of which Brazil is the world's largest exporter. Plans to develop Brazil's vast oil and gas resources will help to reduce the country's large energy bill but the plans are opposed at home and abroad on environmental grounds.

Trade

In the past, primary products such as coffee and soybeans were the main exports. Recently, more money has been made from exporting manufactured goods and chemical products. Major Brazilian imports include machinery and electrical equipment.

Brazil has become self-sufficient thanks to the development of oil-fields offshore, ending decades of dependence on foreign producers. Despite the development of a single market (**Mercosur**) in Latin America, the main export destinations remain the EU and the USA. Most imports come from the EU and USA.

Ordinary Brazilians have benefited from increasing trade because the increased demand for Brazilian goods abroad has led to increased employment, better wages and

Mercosur Countries

Current Members
Applicant Members

Venezuela
Colombia
Ecuador
Peru
Bolivia
Brazil
Chile
Paraguay
Uruguay
Argentina

higher living standards. International trade is vital to Brazil because the money coming in helps to pay off international debt and helps Brazil's development.

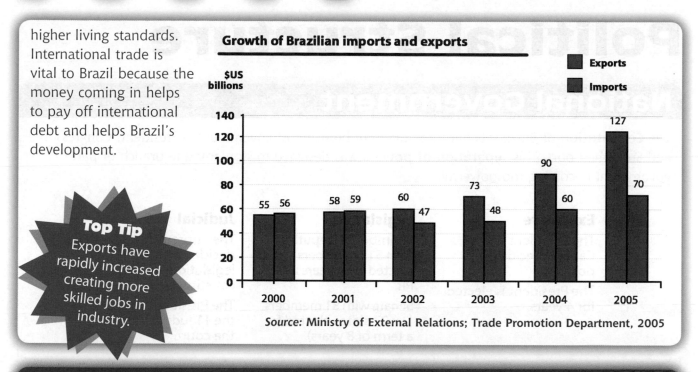

Growth of Brazilian imports and exports

Source: Ministry of External Relations; Trade Promotion Department, 2005

Top Tip
Exports have rapidly increased creating more skilled jobs in industry.

Aid

Given the economic pace at which Brazil is developing, many non-governmental organisations (NGOs) are stepping in to provide aid for vulnerable groups. Aid projects, such as the **Sociedade Civil Mamiraua,** aim to protect the local environment of the rainforest in order to preserve living resources for Natives. This has also helped to reduce poverty and protect the way of life for many Native Indians.

Foreign Debt

Brazil borrowed large sums of money in the 1970s from the **International Monetary Fund (IMF)** and the **World Bank**. Now debt is a growing problem because the government has less money to spend on public services, such as education and healthcare. However, the rich can afford to pay for these services, but the poor cannot.

Campaigners argued that countries could only fully develop if they had the burden of debt lifted and **Jubilee 2000** was a campaign that aimed to do this. However, because Brazil is relatively rich, despite having a high poverty rate, it has not been given as much relief from debt as other countries.

Quick Test

1. In what way do people benefit from increased trade?

2. For what reasons does Brazil face economic problems?

3. What is Jubilee 2000?

4. Explain why inequalities in wealth still exist in Brazil.

Political Structure

National Government

The **Constitution** of Brazil sets out three different branches of government – President, Congress and Supreme Court. This **separation of powers** was designed to stop any one branch or part of government becoming too powerful.

Executive

The President and Cabinet decide on policies.

The President is elected for 4 years.

Legislative

Chamber of Deputies with 513 members elected for 4 years using PR.

Senate with 81 members (3 x 27 states elected for a term of 8 years).

Judicial

The Supreme Court decides whether legislation is constitutional.

The President appoints the 11 judges who sit on the court.

State Government

Each of the 26 states in Brazil has its own government, as does the Federal District of Brasilia, the capital of the country. State government mirrors federal government. Within states there are municipal councils (municipios), run by an elected Mayor, who only deal with local matters.

Top Tip
The next Presidential Election is in 2010.

Presidential Elections 2006

Voting is voluntary for those aged between those aged 16 and 18 and over 70, but it is compulsory for those over 18 and under 70. The turnout of 80% in the 2006 Presidential Election was the highest ever recorded, partly because people from all areas of the country were able to vote **electronically**.

Luiz Inacio Lula da Dilva, President of Brazil

The President of Brazil is **Luiz Inacio Lula da Silva** (known as Lula, pictured right). He is the head of the **Workers Party (PT)**. Lula won the Presidential Election in 2002 with an impressive 62% of the vote and then in 2006 with 60% of the vote. Ordinary Brazilians started to **identify** with Lula who like them had gone hungry, not had enough money, and had worked previously as a shoe-shiner. Lula promised radical **social change**.

Presidential Election Results 2006				
Candidates	**Votes**	**% 1st round**	**Votes**	**% 2nd round**
Luiz Inácio Lula da Silva	46,662,365	48.61	58,295,042	60.83
Geraldo Alckmin	39,968,369	41.64	37,543,178	39.17
Heloísa Helena	6,575,393	6.85	-	-
Cristovam Buarque	2,538,844	2.64	-	-
Ana Maria Rangel	126,404	0.13	-	-
José Maria Eymael	63,294	0.07	-	-
Luciano Bivar PSL	62,064	0.06	-	-
Total	95,996,733	100%	95,838,220	100%

Source: BBC News (Adapted)

Lula's main rival, **Geraldo Alckmin** viewed the first round of the 2006 Presidential Election results as a triumph. He gained strong support in some regions of Brazil, winning 11 of the country's 27 states. He remains popular with wealthy, middle class Brazilians and the business community.

The second round election result, however, showed that Lula still had strong support among many Brazilians. Most of the poor people in Brazil voted for Lula. He won huge victories in poor North Eastern states and also took Minas Gerais and Rio de Janeiro, the country's second and third most populated states.

Quick Test

1. Name the three branches of government in Brazil?
2. For what reasons did people vote for Lula?
3. What are the voting ages in Brazil?
4. What **conclusion** can be drawn from the Presidential election results?

Congress

National Congress

Elections were also held in 2006 for the National Congress. The PT won only around 17% of votes in each house of the Brazilian Congress and therefore lacks a majority government. They have had to form alliances with different parties, giving Congress considerable **power**.

Top Tip
Lack of a majority and weak party loyalty gives the Opposition the upper hand.

2006 National Congress Results				
	Chamber of Deputies		Senate	
Party	Seats	% of Seats	Seats	% of Seats
Workers' Party (PT)*	91	17.7	14	17.3
Democratic Labour Party (PDT)*	21	4.1	5	6.2
Brazilian Labour Party (PTB)*	26	5.1	3	3.7
Brazilian Socialist Party (PSB)*	22	4.3	4	4.9
Brazilian Communist Party (PC do B)*	12	2.3	-	-
Liberal Party (PL)/Social Liberal Party (PSL)*	27	5.3	3	3.7
Popular Socialist Party (PPS)*	15	2.9	1	1.2
Brazilian Democratic Movement Party (PMDB)	74	14.4	19	23.5
Liberal Front Party (PFL)	85	16.6	19	23.5
Brazilian Social Democratic Party (PSDB)	71	13.8	11	13.6
Progressive Party (PPB)	48	9.4	1	1.2
Others	21	4.1	-	-
Total	513	100	100	100

* Members of the Coalition Government

Source: SQA

Political Parties

The relationship within and between parties is fragile. In Lula's coalition government there are parties that are completely at odds with one another. Politicians switch allegiances for personal gain and privilege. Therefore, party loyalty is weak, and Deputies and Senators who belong to the government coalition do not always vote with the government.

Political Issues

Pressure Groups

Businessmen have a powerful voice in national politics and are organised in the Confederação Nacional da Indústria (CNI), the Federação e o Centro das Indústrias do Estado de São Paulo (FIESP) and other state-based bodies. Despite internal divisions, the **trade unions** are a strong political force. The two key union organisations are the Central Unica dos Trabalhadores (CUT) and the Forca Sindical. The **Roman Catholic Church** remains influential and is well represented in Congress. The Conferencia Nacional dos Bispos do Brasil (CNBB), a confederation of Catholic bishops, has played a role in the defence of civil and political rights.

Political Problems

The government is in a weak position due to the fragile **coalition**. Some members of the coalition feel that government policies have not been radical enough and have not improved the socio-economic status of poorer Brazilians.

Allegations of corruption have further weakened the credibility of the government, though not the popularity of the President himself. The status of the PT has diminished because it campaigned as an ethical party and came to power vowing to clean up politics. However, since then the PT, with a minority in Congress, was accused of having paid **monthly bribes** to Congressmen from other parties to secure votes for the government's legislative programme. The PT has also been accused of distributing top jobs in government and state companies to nominees of coalition partners. As a result, senior cabinet members have resigned.

The PT also promised to bridge the gap between the rich and the poor and support landless workers. Many supporters, and members of the Movemento Sem Terra (MST) are deserting the party because the PT has not delivered many of its manifesto promises. The MST is particularly disappointed with the slow pace of land redistribution. They are also critical of the cuts in public expenditure forced on the government by the IMF and World Bank. They hoped that Lula's government would reject **free market economic policies,** like cuts in social spending, and demand greater independence from the IMF.

Quick Test

1. For what reasons do people consider Congress to be in a strong position?
2. Why would President Lula prefer to have a majority government?
3. Why is party loyalty weak in Brazil?
4. Explain why the Brazilian Government faces political opposition?

Human Rights Issues

Street Children

Many people view street children as the source of many problems in cities such as violent crime and so they do not see their lives as being as valuable. Street children are often arrested by the police, imprisoned, and frequently beaten. Street children are the targets of violence because they are involved in drugs and crime. They are often victims of abuse because they have no protection, supervision and support from responsible adults. Businessmen and shopkeepers, who see street children as bad for business, hire **death squads** to kill them.

There are new laws to protect children, and a growing awareness of their plight exists because of media coverage and campaigns by voluntary organisations. **Bolsa Escola** was set up to encourage children to go back to school by giving them money. Charities also play their part in helping street children. **Pastoral do Menor** offers street children training and helps to reintegrate them with their families.

Women

In Brazil, women have been dominated by men because of a traditional macho culture reinforced by society and religion. There is also discrimination in the workplace – women are concentrated in low paid, low skilled work.

Most major cities and towns have established **special police officers** and **women only police stations** to deal with crime of a domestic nature. However, much of the violence against women still goes unreported or ignored because the criminal justice system is dominated by men.

Law and Order

Brazil does not have a national prison system. Prisons are run by the different states, so there are twenty seven prison systems. However, there is one single prison law for the whole country, stating how prisons should be run and detailing the rights and duties of prisoners. Despite this, in many prisons the rights of prisoners are ignored. There are also high levels of **overcrowding** and **violence**, and **corruption** is widespread.

Action has been taken to address the problem of overcrowding in prisons. Dozens of **new prisons** were built throughout the country. In some states, efforts have also been made to reduce the number of people going to prison. In order to tackle the overcrowding problem some states in Brazil are beginning to look at alternatives to prison, such as community service, for some people convicted of a crime,

Indigenous Population

The development of Amazonia is important to the government because of the growth in tourism and the increased agricultural production for export which helping to reduce Brazil's crippling foreign debt. These differing demands have led to conflict.

The incomers, timber exporters and cattle ranchers for multinational companies, have been hostile and **aggressive** to Natives. They view Natives as a barrier to economic progress. The indigenous population has also been plagued by imported diseases like Hepatitis B and D, high exposure to poisonous pesticides used in tomato production, and outbreaks of malaria, TB, yellow fever and skin diseases. Infrastructure projects in the Amazon including **hydroelectric dams** have flooded many areas and displaced thousands of Natives.

The **National Indian Foundation of Health** was set up to tackle disease but its success has been limited as a result of poor funding and staffing. Brazil has invested $1billion (£533 million) in setting up a system for **satellite monitoring** in the Amazon to ensure no illegal activity goes on. In addition, the **Yanomami (Native Indian tribe)** gained land preservation rights with millions of hectares of land now protected from outside activity.

Landless Workers

Landless workers are **victims of violence** and murder by police or landowners' hired hands. The problems of landless workers are an important issue in Brazil because they are the cause of **political unrest**. The **Movemento Sem Terra** has been active in highlighting the unfairness of Brazil's land distribution over a number of years. They have put pressure on the Workers Party (PT) by withdrawing their support. The government has worked to resolve the issue of **demarcation** (dividing the land) of indigenous lands.

Landless workers protesting about land reforms

Quick Test

1. For what reasons are street children victims of abuse?

2. How are women discriminated against?

3. Why are problems of landless workers an important issue in Brazil today?

4. Explain the reasons for **human rights abuses** continuing in Brazil?

Quick Test Answers

Government and Decision Making in Scotland

Page 7

1. The process that gives power from one parliament to another.

2. 1997 referendum results showed Scottish people wanted devolution; just less than three quarters of those who voted wanted it; 63.5% who voted wanted tax varying powers; smaller majority – approximately 10% less wanted tax varying powers.

3. For – Scottish Parliament allows Scottish people to have a greater say in how the country is run; wishes are no longer swamped on devolved issues. **Against** – some people unhappy because they think devolution did not go far enough; want independence.

4. Service provision in areas such as education is different from the rest of the UK; highlighted the need for 'Scottish solutions to Scottish problems'.

Page 10

1. Each voter has two votes; one for a party and one for a candidate.

2. Advantages – electorate have a greater degree of choice – can vote for smaller parties; result is more proportional – more closely reflecting the views of the public. **Disadvantages** – likelihood of no single party having strong enough mandate to take action; some voters may be confused about the difference between Regional and Constituency MSPs.

3. Minority government unlikely to be able to put all their manifesto promises into action; do not have the majority needed to make decisions; will have to approach other political parties for support on an issue by issue basis;

4. Coalitions involve power sharing between two or more political parties – 1999-2007 Labour and Liberal Democrats formed a coalition government. Minority government is when one party does not have commanding share of seats – since 2007 election SNP have held power as a minority government – rely on co-operation of other political parties to pass legislation.

Page 12

1. Power of appointment; running Government – chairing Cabinet; representing the country internationally; leading the largest party in the Scottish Parliament.

2. Plans government strategy; makes decisions; oversees Scottish Government's legislative programme.

3. Provides politically neutral research and advice; manages Government Departments.

4. Scottish Government's power limited by MSPs, First Minister's Question Time, debates and committees; AMS also limits the power of winning party – likely they will run a minority government or go into coalition with another political party.

Page 14

1. Responsible for delivery of local services while ensuring 'best value'; three services provided are – cleansing and environmental health, education and social work.

2. Local councils are aware of the specific needs of local people – they can target specific areas; STV electoral system means that there are three or four councillors elected to each ward – local people can contact a number of representatives for help.

3. UK central Government (Revenue Support Grant), Council Tax, Business Rates and PPP.

4. Funding – each government relies on another for the majority of its funding, Scottish Parliament gets a large proportion of its funding from the block grant, local government receives bulk of its funding from the Revenue Support Grant; **power** – many people would like powers of the Scottish Parliament extended so 'Scottish voice' would have more of an impact on the lives of the Scottish electorate; but some feel extending power would weaken the Union.

Page 16

1. Send letters, use petitions and demonstrate; this influences government who do not want to risk losing voters and do not want bad publicity to damage their image.

2. Newspapers can support one political party – influence readers over time; most people get their political information from television – brings problems to light but impartial.

3. Show Party Election Broadcasts during an election campaign; take part in press conferences that journalists attend; use spin doctors to spread their political message.

4. Pressure groups may break the law to gather media attention, and to pressure Scottish Government into making decisions; pressure groups have too much power – dangerous because they are unelected.

Government and Decision Making in Central Government

Page 19

1. Representing the people, making laws, controlling finance and examining the work of the Government.

2. Select Committees, Question Time, Divisions and the Opposition.

3. Unrepresentative – out-dated working practices and MPs under control of party whip system.

4. Government controls parliamentary time, has majority on committees and in Commons and keeps MPs loyal through whip system.

Page 21

1. Making laws, examining work of the Government, providing independent debate, judicial role – highest court of appeal.

2. Can only delay laws, does not discuss money bills, passes bills that are part of Government's manifesto.

3. Hybrid chamber of 540, elected by PR party list system and appointed by commission, maximum 15 years term, one-third elected/appointed every 5 years.

4. Undemocratic to have members appointed, not elected; membership unrepresentative; concentrates of narrow issues; inbuilt conservative bias.

Page 23

1. **Powers** – Power of appointment, Running government, International role, Majority leader of largest party in Commons, Executive head of Civil Service. **Limits** – Cabinet rivals, backbench revolts, confidence vote, poor Question Time performance, leadership challenge, bad media coverage.

2. Cabinet plans Government strategy, makes decisions, oversees Government's legislative programme, co-ordinates policies of Government Departments, settles disputes between departments.

3. Civil Service provides politically neutral research and advice, manages Government Departments, provides services to public.

4. Prime Minister can appoint, sack or reshuffle other Government Ministers; collective responsibility means Ministers must support; media focuses on Prime Minister.

Page 25

1. Voting; joining and campaigning for a party; standing as a candidate; contacting/lobbying MP; pressure group activity; contacting the media.

2. Helping to form policies; selecting candidates; standing as a candidate; raising money for election expenses; campaigning; encouraging people to vote.

3. **Strengths** – strong single party government, link between MP and constituency, simple to understand, quick result. **Weaknesses** – governments elected with minority support, wasted votes, tactical votes, smaller parties get votes but not seats, Labour or Conservative usually form the Government.

4. Winning party can get their policies through the Commons without relying on votes of other parties; no need to go into coalition and compromise; stable and likely to do full term in office.

Page 26

1. **Highest** – White, over 65, socio-economic group AB. **Lowest** – Ethnic minorities, 18-24, socio-economic group DE.

2. Less interest in politics, voting no longer seen as civic duty, lack of trust in politicians, little difference between parties, result ioften foregone conclusion, inconvenient voting arrangements.

3. Postal, text or computer voting, voting in supermarkets, weekend voting, political advertising, encourage independent candidates by making it harder to lose deposit, compulsory voting, positive abstention, change election system to PR.

4. **Turnout** – Young people, those on benefits and ethnic minorities less likely to vote; white, social class AB, over 65 more likely to; 45% do not vote because not interested or distrust, politicians; **participation** – voting most common form; few take part in political party activity; more are likely to participate in pressure group activity.

Page 28

1. Newspapers can support one political party – influence readers over time; most people get their political information from television – brings problems to light but impartial.

2. The Official Secrets Act to protect sensitive information, Press Code to regulate conduct of the press, suing for slander or libel, laws to limit cross-media ownership.

3. Party Election Broadcasts, press conferences, columns websites, blogs, podcasts, social networking, politicians media trained, spin doctors to handle image.

4. Newspapers not politically neutral; can be biased and support one party; few owners with big influence; little political coverage in tabloids; sensationalise scandals.

Equality in Society – Wealth and Health in the United Kingdom

Page 31

1. Established to address health and wealth inequalities in Britain in 1945 – establishment of many key policies and services, such as the National Health Service.

2. **Relative poverty** – measured by taking into consideration what society considers being normal and measuring it against what an individual has. **Absolute poverty** – life threatening, for example a lack of access to food and shelter.

3. Expanding role of the Welfare State and the cost of providing these services.

4. Different scales and surveys used focus on different aspects of poverty; some focus on income levels; others focus on society's expectations about what a person should have.

Page 33

1. Lack of income impacts on ability to pay for basic necessities essential to everyday life, this will damage an individual's self-esteem.

2. They are often victims of discrimination; other factors can make them vulnerable such as traditional family roles and cultural expectations.

3. Many people living in poverty live in poor quality, run-down housing; housing is likely to be damp, making individuals vulnerable to health problems; these conditions may impact on mental health, increasing likelihood of depression; people living in poverty more likely to smoke and drink excessive amounts of alcohol, both of which can damage health.

4. Social exclusion is a term used to describe a lack of opportunity, income and power; leads to a sense of hopelessness and failure.

Page 35

1. **Universal benefits** – all people, in certain circumstances, are entitled to these; example – Child Benefit; **means-tested benefits** – individuals have to meet certain criteria; example – to claim JSA a person must be actively seeking employment.

2. Phase 1 – work with a personal adviser to write a CV highlighting their skills, qualities and experiences. Phase 2 – voluntary work building experience in a particular area to become more employable.

3. **Financial advantage** – able to afford a basic standard of living while they are actively seeking employment; amount of money entitled to varies depending on family circumstances; **training advantage** – unemployed people have opportunity to develop skills and gain qualifications to them more employable; **employment advantage** – will gain experience in a particular area of work.

4. Working Tax Credits and Child Tax Credits aim to support individuals who make the choice to gain employment rather than claim benefits; Housing Benefit reduces rent for those on low income/benefits.

Page 37

1. Housing will generally be poor quality, with many people exposed to damp – causing conditions like asthma and bronchitis; poor lifestyle choices are more prevalent leading to high levels of disease and low life expectancy.

2. Low income gives people less chance to make good health choices, leading some to have a poor diet and others to abuse alcohol and drugs to escape poverty. These factors can cause health problems such as heart disease and depression.

3. Poverty reduces quality of life – less access to good quality education, private health care.

4. Bodies deteriorate as people age – elderly people over the age of 85 are more likely to suffer from illnesses, such as arthritis, heart disease and hypothermia.

Page 40

1. Advances made in medical technology and medicines – people now have greater expectations of what the NHS can do for them; Britain has an ageing population.

2. **Primary care** – health services that most people use locally, such as doctors and dentists; **secondary care** – long term treatment more likely to involve hospitals.

3. **Community care** – people maintain independence by receiving care in their own home; care designed to meet needs of individual; not always the best option, but is often the cheapest; **residential care** – better for others because the independence of living at home may make them more vulnerable to ill health or injury.

4. People are encouraged to receive care within their own home, they have a personalised care plan drawn up by a social worker and care is provided by social services and communities by home support workers and volunteers.

Page 41

1. Healthy eating programmes in schools discourage pupils from making poor dietary choices – schools no longer sell sweets or fizzy drinks; intended to act as a long term solution to health problems as good lifestyle habits are learned in childhood.

2. Councils ensure all school pupils have access to at least one nutritionally balanced meal a day; reduce the stigma associated with free school meals by using swipe card systems.

3. Providing services that are quick to access for those able to pay for treatment; help meet needs of NHS patients – many new hospitals are built with the private sector in the form of Public Private Partnerships.

4. If people learn good eating habits in childhood they are likely to continue with them as they age; common Scottish health problems like obesity and heart disease will reduce; standard of peoples' lives will improve.

Crime and the Law in society

Page 43

1. Crime is any action that breaks the law and for which someone can be punished.

2. Crimes against the person, crimes against property, 'street' crime, gun and knife crime, white collar crime, corporate crime, organised crime, political crime, minor offences.

3. **Economic** – 'status frustration' and envy, not able to get possessions legally; **social** – family break-ups, different values, peer pressure, deprivation, drug and alcohol abuse.

4. Non-violent crime is most common; motor vehicle offences highest – $1/3$ of recorded offences; dishonesty and vandalism another $1/3$; drugs 4%; crimes of violence 1%.

Page 45

1. **Alcohol** – 18 to buy, local bye-laws ban drinking in public- police can confiscate alcohol, proof of age before sale, drunks refused service, no 'happy hours', illegal to buy alcohol for under-18s. **Tobacco** – advertising, sponsorship and smoking in enclosed spaces banned, 18 to buy, fines for selling to under-18s.

2. **Alcohol** – 21 to buy in supermarkets or off licences, fixed minimum price, ban cheap promotions, 'social responsibility fee' from retailers to pay for cost of misuse; **tobacco** – licence sellers, plain packets, no displays or ten packs, crack down on smuggling and counterfeiting.

3. **For** – fewer places to buy tobacco, increase health benefits, reduce illegal sales to young people because retailer will have to ask for proof of age or risk fine or loss of licence. **Against** – difficult to enforce, smoking not reduced in other countries with licensing, can be obtained illegally and Increase criminal activity like smuggling.

4. **For** – reduce anti-social behaviour by making it more difficult for young teenagers to buy, reduce alcoholism by delaying age can start buying, reduce alcohol fuelled crime, reduce traffic accidents due to drink. **Against** – increase illegal drinking in public, cannot enforce current laws, old enough to marry at 16 but not buy alcohol, lower drinking age and fewer problems in some European countries.

Page 48

1. Offence to possess, supply or intend to supply controlled drug, drugs classified as A, B or C with increasing penalties, cannabis reclassified, assets of convicted drug dealers can be seized, police can enter and close down 'drug dens'.

2. Increase classification of cannabis, target growing and supplying, ban sale of drug taking equipment, harsher sentences for dealing near schools.

3. **For** – reduce number of young people killed in road accidents; stop dangerous driving due to over-confidence, peer pressure, alcohol and drugs. **Against** – reduced mobility in rural areas; difficult to enforce; accidents due to inexperience, not age.

4. **For increase** – 'skunk' three times stronger than ten years ago; use increased; can be addictive; increased convictions for driving under influence; 'gateway' drug. **For reduction** – less harmful than alcohol or tobacco; criminalises medical users; link to mental illness not proved; tough laws not working.

Page 50

1. Stop and question suspect or witness; search someone on suspicion of offensive weapons, stolen property, or terrorism; detain someone at police station for up to 6 hours for questioning; arrest and charge someone seen committing crime; enter building with warrant or without one if pursuing a suspect, hear disturbance or suspect drug den; issue Fixed Penalty Notices.

2. Police can detain terror suspect for up to 28 days without charge, plans to increase this because difficult to gather evidence from computers and abroad.

3. **For** – police and community work together, police get to know local people, people feel safer seeing police on the 'beat', work with social work, education, youth groups, neighbourhood watch. **Against** – relies on public reporting crime and being witnesses, faster response with cars, record and identify more offenders with CCTV, police more specialised, fewer officers available for foot patrols, recruiting difficult.

4. Police protect public, keep law and order, prevent and detect crime, gather evidence, appear in court or Children's Hearings, work with community.

Page 52

1. Looks at evidence gathered by police, decides whether to prosecute, inquires into sudden or suspicious deaths and fatal accidents.

2. Trial without a jury; sheriff, magistrate or JP decides; Justice of the Peace Courts or Sheriff Courts for less serious offences.

3. Trial with jury; Sheriff Courts or High Court for serious crimes.

4. Criminal – Justice of the Peace Courts, summary, hearing minor offences; Sheriff Courts, summary and solemn, hearing more serious offences; High Court of Justiciary summary, hearing most serious offences; Scottish Court of Criminal Appeal hearing appeals from the lower courts; **Civil** – Scottish Land Court and tribunals settling disputes in agriculture, employment, immigration; Sheriff Courts hearing divorce, bankruptcy, eviction; Court of Session Outer House hearing cases involving large sums of money; Court of Session Inner House hearing appeals; House of Lords hearing appeals from Court of Session.

Page 54

1. Custodial – detention in prison or Young Offenders Institution; **non-custodial** – served in the community.

2. Fine, Fixed Penalty Notice, Supervised Attendance Order, Probation, Community Service Order, Restriction of Liberty Order (electronic tagging), Drug Treatment and Testing Order, Community Reparation Order, Anti-Social Behaviour Order.

3. More non-custodial sentences, ending prison sentences of less than 6 months, supervised bail orders, 'conditional sentences', 'progress courts' to review community sentences.

4. For – more appropriate for some types of offences, prison does not rehabilitate, prisons overcrowded, 'revolving door', reoffending rate. **Against** – must have prison where offender is danger to community, prison can rehabilitate and educate, non-custodial not deterrent to crime, 'soft' option, high re-offending rate, cannot offend when locked up.

Page 55

1. Reporter can give advice, arrange for police warning, set up voluntary programme to work on behaviour, refer case to Children's Hearing (Panel).

2. For – keeps under-16s out of adult courts; care and protection, not punishment; reaches young people before criminal stage; supervised programmes deal problems. **Against** – too 'soft'; limited outcomes; rapid turnover of panel members; society different; family disintegration; problems with compliance.

3. Extends ASBOs to 12 to 15 year olds, allows electronic tagging of under-16s, bans sale of spray paint to youths, parenting orders requiring parents to control their children, police powers to disperse gangs of young people causing a 'nuisance'.

4. Those concerned about a young person can contact Children's Reporter who will request reports and decide if child needs to be referred to a Children's Hearing (Panel); Panel of three trained volunteers, Reporter, child, parents or guardian, experts discuss what is best for the child, can decide to place child in children's home, residential school, other secure accommodation, with foster parents or at home under supervision, plan of action devised to help child, reviewed regularly and adapted as needs change.

The Republic of South Africa

Page 56

1. Black Africans – over three-quarters of the population, largest group, 79.6% of the population; **Whites** of European descent – second largest population group, 9.1% of the population; Coloureds/mixed race, 8.9% of population; **Indians/Asians** from colonial past, smallest population group, 2.5% of the population.

2. There are nine provinces in South Africa.

3. Northern Cape – rich in minerals, like copper and diamonds.

4. Apartheid was a political system which gave power to Whites as a ruling group; non-Whites were discriminated against; marriages between Whites and non-Whites were banned; Whites had access to best land and opportunities.

Page 58

1. Many people live in poverty with little education; unable to get a job; climate of fear where many well-off people have invested in expensive security measures; poorer people may take justice into their own hands and end up committing criminal acts.

2. Education is now compulsory but fees are still required; problem for poor families and those with large number of children; South Africa economically vulnerable because many people will not be educated to a high enough standard to achieve a good standard of living.

3. HIV/AIDS – for a long time the government did not provide sufficient sex education programmes for school pupils; did not provide the essential drugs needed by sufferers to help them live a longer, better quality life; malnutrition and lack of access to health care also problems.

4. Lack of access to long term education; lack of skills among the workforce; leads to long term unemployment that will have a huge impact on the economy – may make South Africa less globally competitive.

Page 60

1. GEAR replaced RDP because the targets were far too ambitious and the timescales were far too short.

2. Employment Equity Act and Black Economic Empowerment – both introduced to encourage the majority Black population to become economically active by starting businesses and learning skills to take on senior professional positions; Government encouraged businesses to take responsibility for creating more representative workforce.

3. Affirmative Action – positive discrimination that legislates in favour of Blacks; Employment Equity Act allows employers to discriminate in favour of the Black majority, as well as groups such as the disabled, giving them a better chance of employment.

4. **BEE** – Black South Africans have the appropriate training necessary to hold senior well paid jobs, strengthening the economy and allowing for further investment in health, education, etc; **Employment Equity Act** – legislates for Affirmative Action – ensuring companies have to employ a representative set of employees.

Page 62

1. Giving all the right to be educated, free meal – Mandela Sandwich; Employment Equity Act, Black Empowerment Act to give 'lost generation' access to jobs; building 1 million new homes, improving access to electricity and sanitation, attempting land redistribution; recruiting more Black South Africans into the police force.

2. HIV/AIDS has caused the death of many skilled workers, creating an economic problem; socially, has weakened nation because many children are orphaned; HIV/AIDS will have a ripple effect for many generations; attempts to deal with the problem of HIV/AIDS limited because many people continue to contract the disease despite government education programmes; also criticism of government's limited provision of drugs.

3. White farmers resisted because feel they should not have to give up their land; cost of land redistribution is very high – government have to pay compensation; land rights very hard to prove – many Blacks forced from their land do not have documents to prove they were displaced.

4. **Health** – inequalities led to low average life expectancy; health targets less successfully met – HIV/AIDS and malnutrition still significant problems; government now funding drugs – should mean an improvement in quality of life for those with HIV/AIDS. **Education** – high standard of education equals a higher living standard; education has become two-tier system – those who can afford to pay have access to good schools with decreasing class sizes; significant number of people cannot afford to pay for their children to attend school between the compulsory ages of 7-15;

Page 64

1. National Assembly and National Council of Provinces.

2. There are 400 MPs in the National Assembly.

3. President and Premier only serve two terms to stop them becoming too powerful – making decisions that may only benefit them rather than the people of South Africa; limitation put in place by the South African Constitution in 1996.

4. Constitutional Court ensures proposed legislation will not breach the constitution; acts to protect South African citizens by safeguarding democracy.

Page 66

1. ANC has performed well in all elections since 1994 – gaining larger share of national vote in 2004 than in 1999 or 1994; success repeated in provincial elections and municipal elections – control majority of provinces, dominated 2006 municipal elections.

2. ANC draw their support from Black majority population; people loyal because they are viewed as party who conquered Apartheid; achievements in power on housing, education, health and employment.

3. 76.7% electoral turnout in 2004 – drop of 12.6% from 1999; result of dissatisfaction with speed of social and economic change; some people not seeing point of voting because believe there is no real opposition to the ANC.

4. **Support** – electoral turnout is high; all eligible citizens have right to vote in free and fair elections; South African people have voted for a dominant ANC; South Africans have freedom of expression; **oppose** – lack of real political opposition to ANC; although electoral turnout is high it has declined; traditional voting still race based.

Page 68

1. Only weak political opposition in form of a large number of political parties, but in recent years a stronger opposition has emerged.

2. **ANC** – working towards establishment of a competitive South Africa, where social and economic targets are met and all races are treated equally; **DA** – aim to be non-racial alternative to ANC, addressing social and economic inequalities that, they believe, ANC are not doing enough to solve; **IFP** – aim for greater power sharing between **spheres** of government – National, Provincial and Municipal.

3. COSATU – fights for a democratic, non-discriminatory South Africa.

4. Political opposition is fragmented due to sheer volume of parties who 'split' the vote; significant because while many South Africans are dissatisfied with the progress made by ANC on social, economic and political issues they may not vote for other parties because they perceive them as weak.

The People's Republic of China

Page 70

1. 70% of output now produced by private companies instead of State Owned Enterprises.

2. SEZs' tax incentives boost economy and trade by encouraging foreign companies to invest and produce goods for export. Household Responsibility System means farmers can increase income by selling own crops – workers released for TVEs and urban areas. Allowing rural migrants to register for urban *hukou* makes it easier for workers to move to jobs in urban areas.

3. They own their own homes; have Western fashion, cars and fast foods like McDonalds and KFC, use the internet and watch Western movies and sport on satellite TV.

4. Richest province – 34% of population migrants, high literacy rate, live six years longer, produces consumer electrical goods and clothes for export. **Poorest** – 73% rural, nearly half land is mountain and desert, lower life expectancy and literacy rate, non-consumer mining and petrochemicals.

Page 72

1. Big difference between rich and poor – half population earn 2000 Yuan (£140) a year, but top 4% earn 10 times that amount; big difference between urban and rural – urban income at three times the rural; huge difference between migrant and non-migrant – national average income is eight times the income of an unskilled migrant.

2. End of a job for life – high unemployment among former SOE workers, only those with skills get jobs; end of other social services – poor cannot afford school fees, half urban population and 90% of rural population have no medical coverage from employers, less subsidised state housing, poor cannot afford rising house prices.

3. Crime growing faster than economy; 20% of consumer goods counterfeit, reputation for quality threatened; corruption among officials, reputation for honest business practices threatened.

4. Urban PDI is four times rural; rural unemployment is four times higher; % of population with no education is four times higher in rural areas; 90% of rural population have no health insurance from employers.

Page 74

1. Minimum Living Allowance for people on low incomes; raising level of income at which poorer people start paying tax; taxing 45% of income of the rich, 5-Year Plan target to raise PDI by 30%.

2. CCDI set up 'Ten Taboos' rules, encourages people to report on hotline and website, jails or sentences to death high ranking officials; 'Strike Hard' campaigns target particular crimes and punish harshly e.g. 'Thunderstorm' campaign against counterfeiting.

3. National Project of Compulsory Education in Impoverished Areas provides funds to cover school fees, rural boarding schools; Rural Co-operative Medical Care System – patient pays 10 Yuan a year, government and province divide rest of the cost; 'Go West' Policy encourages foreign firms to poorer Western provinces, vocational schools to develop skills, 5-Year Plan target to transfer 45 million to non-agricultural jobs.

4. >80% coverage by New Rural Cooperative Medical Care System target of 5-Year Plan; pilot for Healthy China 2020 Programme to be extended to provide basic universal health care for all China; crackdown on corruption – head of State Food and Drugs Administration sentenced to death for bribery.

Page 76

1. Recommended by 2 members, checked and tested by local CPC, 2 years probation to join the party; elected by primary party organisation as delegate to local party congress, then to National Party Congress where chosen as member of Central Committee, then Politburo.

2. Top leaders of CPC also provide the Government, same people on Politburo and Standing Committee of State Council, Politburo influences National People's Congress.

3. NPC is China's 'parliament', delegates represent cities, provinces and armed forces, meets annually, chooses President, Vice-President, State Council and Standing Committee that meets every 2 months, makes laws but usually follows Politburo decisions.

4. Member of CPC, primary party organisation and local congress representing party views locally – member of National Party Congress representing views to party leaders; member of Central Committee or Politburo deciding policy for party and Government; standing for local elections for local people's congresses – delegate to National People's Congress making laws and choosing Government leaders – member of State Council running the country of behalf of people and party.

Page 78

1. Direct elections for village committees and local people's congresses on mainland and part of Legislative Councils of Hong Kong and Macao; rest are indirect elections where delegates of one level of party or Government choose the delegates for the next level.

2. Eight registered Democratic Parties registered allowed to operate as long as they share CPC aims; Hong Kong and Macao parties cannot operate in mainland China; all other parties are banned and members are watched.

3. Rich provinces and cities like Guangdong and Shanghai may want more say in running their economic affairs; poorer provinces may want more power to tackle inequalities; wealthy business people may want more influence; gap between rich and poor and Western influence from internet and satellite TV may encourage demand from more democracy.

4. Can only participate in direct elections at village or local congress level; top Government officials appointed, not elected; candidates and top Government jobs mostly limited to CPC members; political parties limited to CPC and 8 approved 'democratic parties'; forming other parties or pressure groups banned; activists monitored, media censored and protests put down.

Page 80

1. Media censored – Law of Guarding State Secrets used to stop criticism – Great Firewall of China blocks internet access – PSB holds Dang'an – State Subversion Law prohibits organising and protesting – police and troops used to stop protests.

2. Only officially recognises five religions – have to register with SARA and follow state version; bans 'cults' like Falun Gong; sees Tibet and Buddhist leader, Dalai Lama, as threat – outlaws Tibetan flag, encourages Chinese migration, puts down protests.

3. Accused do not have right to lawyer, hear evidence against them or speak in own defence; Laojiao without trial; Laogai in harsh conditions; death penalty and harvesting organs of executed; women less important than men – kidnapping; One Child Policy – forced sterilisations and abortions – rich can afford to pay fines.

4. China distrusted because does not protect the rights given in constitution – population monitored by PSB – detention without trial – harsh sentences – Falun Gong and other religions banned – crackdowns in Tibet and Xingiang – strict enforcement of One Child Policy in some areas; possibility that pressure for reform will grow inside China and foreign countries will not invest or will boycott China.

The United States of America

Page 83

1. **Executive** – the President; **Legislative** – Congress, House of Representatives and Senate; **Judiciary** – Supreme Court.

2. **Federal level** – President, members of House, Senators. **State level** – Governor, members of state assembly, state senators.

3. George Bush defeated John Kerry in 2004. In 2008, Barack Obama narrowly defeated John McCain in the popular vote, but won by a majority of the Electoral College votes.

4. State governments make laws on education, health, housing in their state; Federal Government makes laws for whole country on issues like defence.

Page 85

1. Whites, Hispanics (also known as Latinos), Blacks (also known as African Americans), Asian and Pacific Islanders, Native Americans.

2. American Dream, capitalist economic system, democratic government.

3. **For** – contribution to economy; land of the free. **Against** – competition for jobs; strain on welfare services.

4. Blacks in South for historical reasons, moved to urban areas in North for jobs, 'reverse migration' to the South for employment; Hispanics in 'sunbelt states' (Mexicans), Florida (Cubans) and New York (Puerto Ricans) because nearest point of entry; Asian Americans in West because of cultural links.

Page 87

1. Dominated by one ethnic group, poor quality housing, high levels of crime and violence.

2. APIs have greater levels of attainment, lower exclusion rates and higher rates of graduation because they place a greater value on education; Hispanics and Blacks tend to attend schools in inner cities that are starved of resources.

3. Hispanics and Blacks more likely to live in poverty; less likely to have health insurance.

4. Health Savings Accounts increase availability of health insurance by offering tax credits; legislation like Opportunity Scholarship Programme, College Opportunity and Affordability Act providing financial assistance for further education.

Page 89

1. Poorer educational attainment; language difficulties for recent immigrants; English as second language; discrimination and racism; illegal status of some recent immigrants.

2. White flight has meant reductions in welfare spending; vicious cycle of poverty traps people; some employers discriminate against minorities; low political participation; minorities under-represented and their issues have low priority.

3. Economic progress in employment, rise of middle class Blacks, affluent Hispanics setting up their own businesses; APIs done well in education, have higher average income than any other group.

4. **For** – reduces social and economic inequalities; undoes wrongs of previous discriminatory practices; creates more equal society; gives opportunities to Black Americans. **Against** – negative impact on Whites; opposition on basis of discrimination; promotes less qualified individuals.

Page 91

1. Presidents usually male, few female Senators or members of House of Representatives in proportion to number of women in society.

2. Lower social and economic position; lower level of educational attainment; discrimination and prejudice; lower level of involvement in voting; electoral system; financial barriers to involvement; settlement patterns.

3. Redistricting – changing electoral boundaries to create a majority Black electorate.

4. Three distinct candidates at Primary stage, oldest candidate, minority candidate from a major party, female candidate.

Page 93

1. Senators, members of the House of Representatives, President, Governor, Mayor, many state official posts.

2. Motor Voter Law; Unity 04 Campaign.

3. Join; hire professional lobbyists; demonstrate on issues; sign petitions; use media; raise money.

4. Difficulties in registration; little perceived differences between parties; disillusionment with politics/politicians; poor educational attainment; language difficulties; illegal status of some immigrants.

The European Union

Page 95

1. To prevent any further conflict in the aftermath of the Second World War.

2. Single market – no taxes, tariffs or duties on goods exported from one member state to another; freedom of movement – free to live and work in any other member state with full entitlement to social security, benefits, medical care and education.

3. 17% of goods being traded in the European Union and more than a quarter of services.

4. Still differences in VAT, excise duties, taxes on company profits and income tax; move to single currency and full monetary union not completed.

Page 98

1. Increased to twenty five members May 2004; Bulgaria, Romania joined in January 2007; Croatia, Macedonia, Turkey are candidate countries seeking membership.

2. More members therefore more customers for EU goods; firms can sell to bigger market; greater variety of goods to buy.

3. Increases the movement of labour from one country to another e.g. increase in Polish workers settling in the UK; recent estimates suggest decline in number of Poles working in the UK.

4. Majority of budget directed towards cohesion and competitiveness for growth and employment; rest of the budget is divided between other areas including direct aid and rural development.

Page 100

1. Member states within the EU who have adopted the Euro as their currency.

2. No commission for changing money; benefits business; convenient for holiday makers in Eurozone; eliminates cost of transferring the £ into Euros.

3. Member states lose control over the use of monetary policy; cannot change interest rates which are now decided by European Central Bank.

4. When UK Government meets five economic tests will ask electorate in a referendum whether they wish to adopt Euro.

Page 103

1. CAP takes too large a portion of EU budget; EU spending priorities need to be altered to take account of changing nature of EU; reforms have not gone far enough; CAP costly, inefficient and wasteful when pays farmers not to use land or subsidises to compete against farmers from developing countries is wasteful.

2. Special help through Structural funds from European Regional Development Fund, European Social Fund, European Agricultural Guarantee, Guidance Fund, Cohesion Fund to reduce poverty and unemployment, stimulate cooperation and business.

3. Imposes quota on fishermen to allow fish stocks; restrictions on number of days and time of year that boats can fish and controls on size of nets.

4. Nearly half spending directed to France, Spain and Germany; Italy, UK, and Greece also benefit.

Page 105

1. There is still a threat to the peace in Europe. There are still issues needing dealt with following the war in Iraq and terrorism continues to be a threat since Sept 11.

2. NATO can intervene in various trouble spots that continue to exist around Europe. Threats to Europe from around the world are increasing (e.g. threat from terrorists following September 11th, Madrid and London bombings, 2005).

3. Arguments for include: making the alliance stronger and being able to act against international terrorism. Arguments against include: difficulties in coordinating actions across all member states and relying on outdated equipment.

4. EU military involvement has taken place in partnership with NATO in countries such as Afghanistan. The EU has also taken part in peacekeeping missions in the Democratic Republic of Congo.

Development in Brazil

Page 107

1. Differences exist in population, area, climate, agriculture and industry.

2. Whites, Blacks and Mixed Race.

3. Moqueca is a popular food and coffee is a popular drink.

4. Differences exist because of economic factors such as employment, industry and income; South East has greater strength in industry, grows many cash crops, has higher population generating greater income; North relies on agriculture and Amazon for employment.

Page 109

1. Poor quality, overcrowded housing, high levels of crime, few amenities.

2. Inequalities exist in enrolment, attendance and qualifications between regions and ethnic groups.

3. Police corruption and violence, availability of guns and drugs deters tourism, health care costs as a result of violence.

4. Brazilian Government introduced social programmes such as Fome Zero to ensure poor Brazilians had access to food; also creation of the Ministry of Cities has improved living conditions by providing sewerage and sanitation facilities for those living in favelas.

Page 111

1. People benefit from increased trade; increased employment creating better living standards.

2. Brazil faces economic problems because of the high level of inequalities, the level of foreign debt and uneven regional development.

3. Jubilee 2000 was a pressure group that campaigned for reductions in debt.

4. Unequal ownership of land has meant that landowners have greater wealth; inequalities in education have led to an unskilled workforce with low pay; economic policies as a result of debt have meant cuts in spending.

Page 113

1. Executive made up of the President and Cabinet; Legislative made up of Congress; Judicial branch made up of the Supreme Court.

2. Ordinary Brazilians identified with Lula' considered him to be like them; his party promised radical social change and a reduction in inequality.

3. Voting is voluntary for those aged between those aged 16 and 18 and over 70, but it is compulsory for those over 18 and under-70.

4. First round of elections were close but Lula secured victory in the second round of elections with a clear majority.

Page 117

1. Congress in a strong position; can stop legislation going through the Senate and Chamber of Deputies because coalition parties do not have a majority.

2. He would prefer a majority government so that he can get his policies through Congress without relying on votes of other parties.

3. Party loyalty is weak as the result of bribes and corruption.

4. Nature of coalition means that a number of parties will compete for power; allegations of corruption have eroded the credibility of the party; MST resistance to government inaction; IMF constraints.

Page 119

1. Negative attitude of the police, shop owners and a lack of protection from family may result in street children being victims of abuse.

2. Women earn less, face sexual discrimination and are concentrated in low status work.

3. Cause of political unrest, violence and killings, unemployment and growth in favelas.

4. Economic constraints; problems in the criminal justice system; deeply entrenched social attitudes; costs of fixing problems.

Websites for Intermediate Modern Studies

Links to all these websites can be found on the Leckie and Leckie Learning Lab. **http://www.leckieandleckie.co.uk/**

Government and Decision Making in Scotland

Scottish Parliament
Intermediate Modern Studies resources with information on functions of the Scottish Parliament, job of an MSP, how laws are made, committees and pressure group participation.

The Lawmakers, BBC Scotland Education
Interactive guide to lawmaking in Scottish Parliament, including role of pressure groups.

Holyrood TV
Live streaming and archive footage from the Scottish Parliament.

Vote Scotland, Electoral Commission
Elections results, how AMS and STV voting systems work, how to vote animated video and voting games.

Scotland's Politics, BBC News
Up-to-date news stories, political guides and videos.

Local Government, BBC Scotland Education
Information, activities and investigations on the work of local government and councillors.

Profile of Scotland, BBC News
Information on leaders, media and links to other websites.

Government and Decision Making in Central Government

UK Parliament
Up-to-date information on what Parliament is doing, links to House of Commons and House of Lords websites and interactive guide to the work of Parliament.

No10, Prime Minister's Office
Information and videos on work of the Prime Minister.

UK Parliament TV
Live streaming, archives and videos of work of House of Commons and House of Lords.

Electoral Reform Society
Information on how election systems work, alternative voting methods and election results.

Politics, BBC News
Up-to-date news stories, political guides and videos.

Profile of the United Kingdom, BBC News
Information on media, leaders and links to other websites.

Equality in Society: Wealth and Health in the United Kingdom

Wealth and health inequalities, BBC Scotland Education
Interactive guide with information, case studies and exercises on wealth and health inequalities.

Healthier Scotland, InfoScotland
Links to information about current health campaigns and changes to the law.

Crime and the Law in society

Scottish Courts
Information on the court system in Scotland.

Scottish Police Service
Information and crime statistics for each police force in Scotland.

Scottish Police Services Authority
Information about Scottish Crime and Drug Enforcement Agency, Forensics Service and links to other websites.

Criminal Justice in Scotland
Links to newspaper articles about criminal justice.

Children's Hearings, Scottish Government
Information about Children's Hearing System.

Anti-Social Behaviour, Scottish Government
about anti-social behaviour and the law.

InfoScotland, Scottish Government
Links to information about drugs, alcohol, tobacco and road safety.

The Republic of South Africa

Profile of South Africa, BBC News
Information on leaders, media and links to other websites.

South Africa, BBC Scotland Education
Step-by-step interactive guide to politics, economic and social issues in South Africa.

South Africa – Country briefing, The Economist
Factsheets on South Africa and links to articles and other websites.

The People's Republic of China

Profile of China, BBC News
Information on leaders, media and links to other websites.

Changing China, BBC News
Background information, features and up-to-date news about China.

How China is ruled, BBC News
Clickable diagram and information on how China is governed.

China – Country briefing, The Economist
Factsheets on China and links to articles and other websites.

China Daily
Articles about economy, politics and life in China.

Human rights in China
Pressure group campaigning on human rights issues in China.

The United States of America

Modern Studies – USA, BBC Scotland Education
Information and case studies about how America is governed.

Guide to the US Government, BBC News
Clickable diagram and information on how the USA is governed.

United States – Country briefing, The Economist
Factsheets on United States and links to articles and other websites.

The European Union

Profile of European Union
Information on leaders, media and links to other websites.

Inside Europe, BBC News
Information about European Union and links to television programmes and other websites.

Development in Brazil

Profile of Brazil, BBC News
Information on leaders, media and links to other websites.

Brazil – Country briefing, The Economist
Factsheets on Brazil and links to articles and other websites.

Index